Chicken
Poop
for the
Soul
II

D0068023

Also by David Fisher

Chicken Poop for the Soul

Published by POCKET BOOKS

For orders other than by individual consumers, Pocket Books grants a discount on the purchase of **10 or more** copies of single titles for special markets or premium use. For further details, please write to the Vice President of Special Markets, Pocket Books, 1230 Avenue of the Americas, 9th Floor, New York, NY 10020-1586.

For information on how individual consumers can place orders, please write to Mail Order Department, Simon & Schuster Inc., 100 Front Street, Riverside, NJ 08075.

Chicken Poop

for the Soul II

More Droppings

A parody by
David Fisher

POCKET BOOKS
New York London Toronto Sydney Singapore

This book is a work of fiction. Names, characters, places and incidents are products of the author's imagination or are used fictitiously. Any resemblance to actual events or locales or persons, living or dead, is entirely coincidental.

An *Original* Publication of POCKET BOOKS

POCKET BOOKS, a division of Simon & Schuster Inc.
1230 Avenue of the Americas, New York, NY 10020

Copyright © 2000 by David Fisher

All rights reserved, including the right to reproduce
this book or portions thereof in any form whatsoever.
For information address Pocket Books, 1230 Avenue
of the Americas, New York, NY 10020

ISBN: 0-671-03708-0

First Pocket Books trade paperback printing August 2000

10 9 8 7 6 5 4 3 2 1

POCKET and colophon are registered trademarks of
Simon & Schuster Inc.

Cover design by Brigid Pearson; front cover photo by PhotoDisc

Printed in the U.S.A.

John D. Rockefeller once said that the greatest gift a man can have is a friend he can bank on. So, with great humility I would like to dedicate this book to someone who has been a true and loyal friend, one of the great human beings, someone I love and admire very deeply, my very close friend _____.

(Fill in Your Name Here)

Acknowledgments

There are several people without whom this poop would not be possible. My publisher and editor, Emily Bestler, who understood the world needs laughter—yet still published this book. Her assistant editor, Kip Hakala, the first person to have taught me the very important lesson that the dot goes after his *first* name in an e-mail address. Jesse and Beau Stevens, Alex and Jordan Langsam, and Noah Glenn, who leave me no option but to laugh. And I remain eternally grateful to my wife, Laura, for her suggestions, her patience, her support, and her insistence that I get out and exercise.

Contents

CONTENTS

Three Little Words

I HAD REACHED THE SUMMIT OF MY MIDLIFE CRISIS. I FELT STUCK in a deep rut, going nowhere, looking forward to nothing. I knew that if I didn't try to change my life, I was doomed to decades of repeating my same old mistakes. But I didn't how to make those changes—until I read a wonderful book of inspirational stories. A woman from St. Louis, Missouri, wrote that she had changed her life simply by telling people that she loved them. People responded to those three little words in wonderful ways, and since that time her life had been greatly fulfilled. So I decided to try it myself. I vowed that for one day I would tell each person I met that I loved them.

I began the next morning while sitting at the small kitchen table with my wife of eighteen years. It had been a long time since I'd expressed any real feelings toward her. The truth is we had been going through some rough times; we'd even discussed separating. So I took a deep breath, cleared my throat, and said it: "I love you."

A change immediately came over her. She put down her coffee and looked at me quizzically. Then she responded with three little words of her own: "Are you nuts?"

But by the time I got to my office I was excited. I had made real contact with my life. I had changed the dynamics of my relationship with my wife. In mid-morning I called my young secretary into my office. She'd been with me for almost a year, and she was a terrible secretary. She forgot phone calls, she didn't finish her work, she was often late to the office and left early. I had been tough with her and I knew she didn't like me much. So as she stood in front of my desk, once again I got up my courage and said those three little words: "I love you."

She was absolutely stunned. Her arms dropped to her side and she shook her head. And then she responded with three little words of her own: "That's sexual harassment."

Later that afternoon I was called into the office of the company's director of human resources. He was a stern, distant man. He was known for being extremely officious and almost obsessively neat. As he started explaining to me why under current corporate guidelines I had committed a legal offense and was therefore being terminated, I interrupted him and said flatly, "I love you."

He looked at me as if he had never seen me before and gulped. Clearly he did not know what to say. Finally, he looked around the room and whispered three little words of his own: "Meet me later."

My desk was cleaned out and I was escorted off the premises by four o'clock that afternoon.

I knew I had to persist. I saw a woman standing by herself, leaning against a building. She looked so alone, so forlorn, that I felt I had to approach her. I had to make contact with her, just one human being to another. So I walked right up to her and said clearly those three little words: "I love you."

And she responded with three little words of her own: "You're under arrest." She pulled out a badge and identified herself as a member of the vice squad.

While this was not turning out precisely as it had in that inspirational book, it certainly was changing my life. As I was brought into the courthouse to be arraigned, a man sat next to me. "I love you," I said.

He laughed, then replied with three little words: "I'm your lawyer."

Finally I was standing before the judge. After listening to my attorney explain the situation, the judge asked me if I had anything to say. Now, how could I possibly resist? "I love you," I said.

He smiled kindly. "Go to jail."

After being released on bail, I took a taxicab home. "I love you," I told the driver.

"Twenty-eight bucks," he said, reading the meter.

The house was dark. But as I turned on the lights, I saw a note on the table. It was from my wife. As I read her note, I knew I had reached her in a way I'd never before thought possible. For on that piece of paper she had written in big, bold letters the three little words I had been longing to hear for so long: "I'm leaving you!"

I had successfully changed my life.

—*Barry Nevell*

A Great Complaint!

This column, written by nationally syndicated advice columnist Dr. Laura Stevens, provoked a lot of good-natured controversy:

Dear Readers: The following letter and my response certainly did stir you up!

Dear Dr. Laura, I love my wife very much, but she is the worst complainer I have ever seen. She complains about everything and everybody. Nothing is good enough for her. When we eat in a restaurant, she always sends her food back; waiting at a traffic light drives her crazy; every movie is terrible and the tickets cost too much; and I can never do anything right at all. From the first thing in the morning to the last thing at night, she tells me I am dumb, stupid, ignorant, lazy, no-account, birdbrain, miserable, boring, selfish, and just about anything else she can think of. I hate to complain, but I can't take it too much longer. How do I change things?

Bobby S, California

Dear Bobby, You are a lucky man! According to the *New England Journal of Medicine*, a five-year study recently concluded in Birmingham, England, indicated that complaining is good for us! People who actively voice their complaints rather than keeping them inside tend to live longer, healthier lives. The study showed that people who complain more than ten times daily live up to four years longer, and it appears that the more they complain the longer they live! While surprised doctors can't explain the reasons for this, they believe it is related to the relief of stress. So by making you complain, your wife is actually doing you a big favor—and helping insure that you'll be there to listen to *her* complaints for many more years. Congratulations!

Many readers took me to task for my response. A small sample:

Dear Dr. Laura, Your response to Bobby S in California was about the dumbest thing I have ever read! The guy's life is a living hell and you're telling him it's been extended? What's wrong with you? Have you completely lost your senses? You're a psycho. Where did you get your doctor's license? Some kids' play-doctor kit? You're a menace to mental health!

Jeff H, New York City

Dear Jeff, Nice complaint! Glad I could help.

Dear Dr. Laura, I have been a loyal reader for fifteen years, and in all that time your response to Bobby S in California is the most ridiculous thing you've ever written! You ruined my day.

Sylvia F, St. Paul, Minnesota

Dear Sylvia, Feel better? It's amazing how well it works, isn't it? Write again soon.

Dear Dr. Laura, When I read the letter from Bobby S in California I knew just how he felt. My wife is also an inveterate complainer. Your response has helped me accept her as she is and cope with this problem, and I'm just writing to thank you.

Steve B, Seattle

Dear Steve, I'm sorry you feel that way. That's not very healthy. Please write again when you feel worse about this problem. Until then I'm worried about you.

There it is, readers. If anything I've written today makes you so angry or upset you want to write to me to complain—you're very welcome! That'll just give us more years to spend together!

—Dr. Laura

Real Country

THE MUSIC WAS BORN IN THE TUMBLEWEEDS AND GREW UP IN the dusty streets. It was no more beautiful than a broken-down Chevy, but real as a dollar bill. All that it ever required was a guitar or a fiddle and an assembly of emotion. More than any other, country music was the music of life. It was the song of the broken heart and the mending spirit. Listening to it on a moon-filled night with the scent of love on the wind was enough to bring tears to the eyes of the big men.

The words came from real life. It reflected all the joys of everyday living: lovers abandoned, women scorned, men betrayed, folks dying, children lost. But as the nation grew into one large shopping mall and country music became popular, the disconnection between the singers and their songs grew wider than the great Missouri. It was singer Marty McDonald who brought the music back to its roots. Real Country, he called it, and it reflected the true problems faced by the modern country singer. The hope and despair of his first record, *Goin' to Nashville to Git Me a Multimillion-Dollar Contract 'Stead a Gettin' a Real Job,* touched a nerve among listeners and became an immediate hit.

His follow-up, *Goin' for the Ole Gold Record,* established him as a major star, and the songs that came after that paralleled his growth as an artist: *He's a No-Accountant Man in an IRA World; Mr. Wall Street Broker Man; I Got More Gals Than You Do;* and *I Got Me a $95,000 Sports Car* resounded with the angst of success.

But unlike many other stars who lost contact with their fans once they became successful, McDonald maintained a strong connection, writing songs especially for them such as *Visit My Official Web Site McD@McD.com Blues; Y'All Call 1-800-111-8787 for McSouvenirs;* and *Help This Album Go Platinum.*

Stardom did not come without heartbreak for Marty McDonald. While other country stars tried to keep their personal life private, true to the new traditions of Real Country, McDonald used it as the basis for his music. His incredibly sad song *My Baby's Got Herself a Palimony Lawyer* became an instant classic; *Too Many Gals Wanna Use Me Up* shot to the top of the charts, as did his mournful dirge *The Price of Fuel for My Jet Keeps A-Risin'.* His laments *My Agent's Takin' 40% and I'm So Sad* and *The Mortgage Man Wants My Mansion* received tremendous radio play.

But McDonald overcame those incredible problems and became bigger than ever, once again celebrating his success in music. From this period came such wonderful songs as *Me and My Pal Bill Gates Down on the Riverbank; Only Supermodels Need Apply; Got Those Insider Tradin' Bucks;* and *My Own Sweet Texas Mall.*

Where does Marty McDonald go from here? That's the question his millions of fans have asked—and perhaps he hinted at the answer in his recently released Real County single *Je Suis le Monde*. Only time will tell.

—*Armand Brescia*

American Institute of Cryogenics, Inc.

kles	Johnson	Peters	**DISNEY**	Tiuk	Mane
ers	Smith	Frank	Lorenz	Kelly	Rom
ameson	Jones	Wallace	Scott	Bost	Goldst

DISNEY ON ICE

Amazing But True! The Incredible Similarities Between Abraham Lincoln and Jim Carrey

FEW PEOPLE WOULD COMPARE THEM, BUT ABRAHAM LINCOLN, the sixteenth president of the United States, and Jim Carrey, Academy Award nominee for Best Actor, have much more in common than anyone would suspect. It's amazing but true.

- Both Abraham Lincoln and Jim Carrey were born to a mother *and* a father!
- Both Lincoln and Carrey were born on the *same* continent in the *same* millennium!
- Lincoln was eventually followed by a president named Truman, while Carrey once played a character named . . . Truman!
- Both Abraham Lincoln and Jim Carrey had beards, except for Jim Carrey!
- Both Abraham Lincoln and Jim Carrey were married to their first wife!
- Abraham Lincoln was a lawyer, Jim Carrey played a lawyer in *Liar Liar!*

- Abraham Lincoln went to Congress in 1847 as a Whig; in his picture *The Mask* Jim Carrey wore a wig!
- Neither Abraham Lincoln nor Jim Carrey graduated from high school!
- Neither Abraham Lincoln nor Jim Carrey ever served a single day in the U.S. Senate or won an Academy Award!
- Both Lincoln and Carrey were taller than six feet yet shorter than seven feet!
- After being shot, Lincoln was carried across the street, while Carrey has often been driven in a Lincoln limousine!
- No one had ever heard of either Abraham Lincoln or Jim Carrey until they became famous!
- Both Abraham Lincoln and Jim Carrey drank spring water from the United States of America!
- Neither Lincoln nor Carrey ever saw a motion picture made by the other one!
- The first name of both Lincoln and Carrey end in the letter *m*, while neither of their last names end in the letter *e*!
- Abraham Lincoln was shot in the dark; Jim Carrey saw the motion picture *A Shot in the Dark!*
- Jim Carrey's first television appearance was on a show entitled *The Duck Factory*, while in Abraham Lincoln's last public appearance he forgot to duck!
- Abraham Lincoln was born in 1809; Jim Carrey was born exactly 153 years later!
- Abraham Lincoln freed the colored slaves, Jim Carrey starred on the TV program *In Living Color!*
- Lincoln's father's first name was Thomas, his mother's maiden name was Hanks; Jim Carrey is a close personal friend of actor Tom Hanks!
- Abraham Lincoln was cast forever in marble, Jim Carrey was cast in *Batman Forever!*

—*Kip Hakala*

Call Me Clumsy

The old adage, "If at first you don't succeed, try, try, again," should not be applied to bungee jumping!

—Jason Klurfeld

They called me Clumsy because I was always tripping and falling and dropping things and spilling things. And for a long time I really hated it. That nickname made me self-conscious. But there was nothing I could do about it. The truth is, I am clumsy and I always have been. I come from a family of clumsy people. As my mother often said, "Clumsy is as clumsy—whoops." And then she'd just go bouncing down an escalator.

Thanksgiving was always the most dangerous night of the year at our house. The whole family would be there. One year I'll never forget my mother tripped over our dog, Bruiser, and spilled the whole gravy boat on the floor. My brother Bump slipped on it and, as he was going down, grabbed the tablecloth and pulled it off the table, causing the turkey to fall right into the lap of my uncle Tripp.

Everybody in my family was clumsy. We were the only family I knew who would get holiday cards "from your friends in the emergency room." We had so many accidents that negligence lawyers offered us retainers.

12

My mother knew that I felt bad about the names the other kids called me. "It's not so terrible," she told me, "you can use it for your own—ow!"

I guess I was in third grade when I finally began to understand what she meant by that. I was on the playground when this kid started calling me clumsy. At that point I was still in denial. "I am not clums—" I said, and then fell off the jungle gym right on top of him. I broke his arm.

I was really afraid I was going to get into terrible trouble, but the teacher had seen everything. "It's okay," she reassured me, "I saw what happened. I know it was an accident. It's not your fault."

That was the first time I heard those lovely words "It's not your fault." And it really wasn't my fault. I couldn't help the things that happened to me, and if I couldn't prevent them, I certainly could not be responsible for them. I began to understand that so long as people understood that I was just naturally clumsy, I could even help accidents happen and still escape blame.

So it wasn't my fault when I couldn't do the homework I hated because my books accidentally fell into a big puddle. And it wasn't my fault in chemistry when those bottles of acid dropped on my term project completely destroying it. And it wasn't my fault when I couldn't take gym because I fell and badly bruised my leg.

As I got older, I embraced my clumsiness. Fortunately, I found the perfect job: I became an examiner at Good Housekeeping's product-testing laboratory. For the first time, being clumsy was a virtue. At the laboratory I broke all the records, but fortunately they had backed them up on the computer.

The only thing that did not go well for me was my social life. Every time I met someone I liked, I would accidentally poke her in the eye or drop something on her foot; one relationship ended when I got my girl-friend's long hair tangled in my electric toothbrush. Once while moving a chair I put it down on the girl's toe and broke it. Another relationship ended when I slammed a refrigerator door on a long fingernail, breaking it. I'm the only man I ever knew who kissed a woman hard enough to break her lip.

Then I met a very special woman. I really liked her a lot. I was terrified that as soon as she found out that I suffered from clumsiness she would end the relation-ship. But then one day as we were walking down the street, she looked up at me with love in her eyes and said, "I have something I need to tell you. I'm really falling for you." And then she did.

I knew at that moment I had met the girl of my dreams.

Call us Clumsies.

—*Jake Richmond*

Déjà View

MY FRIENDS USED TO CALL ME A PROFESSIONAL SKEPTIC. I JUST didn't believe in things I couldn't see with my own eyes. I didn't believe in the supernatural, I have no superstitions, I thought parapsychology was pure hokum. I didn't believe in spirits, or that people could predict the future. I didn't believe in witchcraft or voodoo. I didn't believe out-of-body travel was possible or that people could communicate their thoughts telepathically. I didn't believe in auras, I never read my own horoscope, and I'm not the slightest bit superstitious. I never saw a miracle and I certainly never believed in reincarnation.

Until that day in Minneapolis.

The idea that possibly I had lived before as another person in another time seemed completely ridiculous to me. Scientifically it made absolutely no sense. Certainly, like other people I had experienced moments of déjà vu, when for an instant it felt as if I had lived that moment previously, but I had never experienced anything like I did one winter's day in Minneapolis.

I was there for a business meeting. The meeting took much of one morning, and I had almost a full day to walk around the city. I decided first to grab a quick lunch. I walked into a McDonald's and looked around. *And I knew I had been there before!* I had never set foot in Minneapolis before, yet everything about that McDonald's was familiar. As I looked around, I knew I had seen all the posters and trays and wrappings and tables; even the straws seemed familiar. I felt a chill run down my spine.

I practically ran out of there and found myself in a nearby mall. The first place I entered was a clothing store, The Gap. I am sure I had never been in that store before—yet I knew every single thing they were selling! Somewhere deep inside me I knew I had been there before. But that wasn't possible. It was then the thought occurred to me: I had been there before, but not as me. At least not the me I saw reflected in the mirror that I knew would be hanging in the dressing room.

I took a deep breath. I knew this couldn't really be happening to me. As I left that store, a clerk smiled at me and said, "Have a nice day." And I had known, I had absolutely known, she was going to say that before she did. Somewhere, in the recesses of my past, I had heard those words before.

I was getting really nervous. I decided the best thing to do was duck into a movie theater. A brand-new Meg Ryan-Hugh Grant movie was playing, a romantic comedy. It had just been released. It wasn't possible that I had seen it. Yet as I watched, incredible as it might seem, I knew every single thing that was going to happen in that movie before it happened! I knew she didn't like him at first, and I knew she would eventually warm to him and they would end up together. I knew Hugh Grant would trip and hurt himself, causing her to fall for him. The plot unfolded exactly as I had known it would.

I was terrified. How could this be happening to me? I decided to check into my hotel and lie down. I got into a taxi and . . . and even before I got into that cab I knew the driver was from Eastern Europe. I checked into my hotel and opened the door and looked around . . . and I couldn't move. I had been in that room before. Everything in that room, from the white cotton bed throw with little white balls on it to the faux-wood, brown desk, from the painting of the red barn hanging above the bed to the tiny on-off knob on the lamp, was familiar to me. Everything.

I lay down gently on the bed and dared to turn on the television set. I was so nervous I couldn't concentrate on one thing, so I went from one cable station to the next—and while intellectually I know this was impossible, I felt certain I had seen every single program they were showing. On an interview show I knew that the panel would consist of Arianna Huffington, Alan Dershowitz, Pat Buchanan, and the Reverend Jerry Falwell even before they appeared!

I kept the lights on all night; I was afraid to go to sleep. I have no logical explanation for what happened that day. I don't tell people about it because I doubt they would believe me. And I have no way of proving any of it. But it happened, just as I have described it. And for me, at least, there could be only one explanation: impossible as it might seem, I had been in that place before. And that was the day I started believing in reincarnation.

—*Noah Glenn*

Finding the Good in People

"WE'RE ALL DIFFERENT," MY FATHER OFTEN TOLD ME, "THAT'S probably the only thing we all have in common." My father wasn't famous, he never made a lot of money, but when he left my brothers and me, he gave us one of the greatest gifts of all, the ability to find the good in all people.

My father was always able to find the good in people. The same people whom others considered half-wits, my father considered half-smarts! Big or small, rich or poor, every race, creed, and religion, my father always found something for which to value every human being.

When I was still a young boy, I remember, my dad and I were walking through the parking lot of a local mall when I saw a person with no legs struggling to get out of his car. While I tried not to stare at him, it was impossible. I'd never seen a severely disabled person before.

My father noticed me looking at him and said quietly, "I know that gimpy guy may look really strange to you, but let me tell you something. There's a lot more to that man than his disability."

"What do you mean, Pa?" I asked.

"It's simple. When you see someone like that, you immediately know he's got a handicapped parking sticker for his car. So if you're nice to him, he might let you use it one day so you don't have to park so far away from the stores."

I'd never thought about a handicapped person that way before. I wondered, were there more things that I was overlooking by rushing to judgment about people? That question was answered for me only a week later. My dad and I were walking downtown when we were approached by a homeless man. This man was filthy, his teeth were rotten, his dirty clothes emitted a dank odor. He scared me and I hid behind my father for protection. When that man was gone, my father bent down and looked me right in the eye and said, "Now, son, there's no reason to be afraid of people like that. Sure he was dirty and he smelled like a foot, but if you just took the time to look a little deeper, you would have seen his real value."

I wondered what Dad meant. To me, he was just another homeless man in a city of strangers. When I asked, my father explained, "Suppose you were traveling on the subway and you got lost. Or you were walking along and you couldn't find the street you were looking for? Who would you ask for directions?"

I began to understand what he meant. "You mean . . . ?"

"That's right. Homeless people are much more valuable than street signs. A guy like that guy probably lives on the train. All you saw when you looked at him were his dirty clothes, but to me, a guy like that is a walking map."

I began to understand what he meant. It was not too many weeks later that we saw an extremely fat person walking down the street. To me, this person was almost as big as a house. My father saw my reaction and said softly, "I know, son, you look at that person and you see a big fat tubo'lard, but let me ask you—"

"I know, Pa," I interrupted. "If I was looking for a good place to eat, who would be a better person to ask than a big fat man?"

My father smiled proudly. "That's right son."

Several days later my oldest brother and I saw a blind man carrying a cane walking down the street. Only a few weeks earlier we probably wouldn't have even noticed him. But this time we stopped to stare. "Boy," my brother said, looking perplexed, "I know Dad's right. I know that guy's got to be good for something, but I just can't figure out what."

I knew then that my father had taught me well. "Suppose your TV set breaks down," I explained wisely, "and the only thing you have in your house is a radio, but you have no idea what shows are on what station . . ."

My father's been gone a long time now. But I've never forgotten the lesson he taught me, and I've always been able to find the real value in people.

—*Gerald Simon*

The Secret of Speed Reading

READ FAST.*

*average reading time 2.1 seconds

The Good Teacher

AFTER HIGH SCHOOL HISTORY TEACHER JESSICA REICHLER HAD read several reports criticizing American students for their lack of knowledge about history, she finally felt compelled to speak out. "A lot of teachers haven't realized it yet," she objected, "but most students are also human beings. The fact that they don't know anything about history isn't their fault, it's the fault of their teachers. We have failed to find ways to reach them."

To remedy that situation Reichler developed a history curriculum aimed directly at the modern teenager. Described as "knowledge-based learning," it is based on her conviction that "the best way to teach history is to use what teenagers already know about the present." Examples of questions from several recent tests illustrate this unique approach to learning.

The Declaration of Independence was signed 223 years before the release of the Backstreet Boys album entitled *Millennium*. When was the Declaration of Independence signed? _____

In 1803 the United States purchased 600 million acres of land from France, doubling the size of the nation, for $15 million. Named for the state that would eventually be the birthplace of Britney Spears, this was known as the _____ Purchase.

Brad Pitt's first major role came as the boyfriend of Priscilla Presley's daughter on the television show named after the city in which President John F. Kennedy was assassinated in 1963. John F. Kennedy was shot in _____

The first delegate of the United States to the United Nations was former First Lady
(a) Cindy Crawford (b) Madonna (c) Eleanor Roosevelt (d) Neve Campbell _____

The Treaty of (city where Jim Morrison is buried) _____ ended the Spanish-American War and gave the United States possession of (island where Ricky Martin was born) _____.

Gavin Rosedale is the lead singer of this grunge band that shares the same name as the president of the United States during the Gulf War, George Herbert Walker _____.

Who am I? My first name is the same as that of the actor who plays Dawson on *Dawson's Creek*. My last name is the same as that of the actress who plays Andie on the same show. I'm the fifth president of the United States. Call me _____.

The '49ers raced to California in 1849 after this mineral (a record given to singers for selling a million albums) was discovered in what became known as the _____ rush.

To end the Civil War in 1865, Confederate commander Robert E. (Pamela Anderson . . .) _____ surrendered at the courthouse at Appomattox to Union commander Ulysses S. (Elizabeth Hurley's boyfriend Hugh . . .) _____.

For her efforts, Jessica Reichler was given *Seventeen* magazine's prestigious Teacher We'd Most Like to Take to a Puff Daddy Concert of the Year award.

—*Jessa Holz*

Young Dr. Kevorkian

Until you've walked a mile in another man's shoes,
you have no idea how painful blisters can be.

—Doug Kime

THE WORLD KNOWS HIM AS DR. DEATH, THE CREATOR OF "medicide," the name given to the extremely controversial branch of medicine that offers assistance to terminally ill patients who choose to end their life. But little is really known about the world's most controversial "obitiatrist," Jack Kevorkian, and how he developed his fascinating avocation.

Black Jack, as his friends called him, grew up on a dead-end street in the small town of Gravely, Illinois. In junior high school he was very popular. "Oh, like all kids he had a few enemies," remembers classmate Mary Hayes. "There were these two kids who gave him some trouble, but one day they just moved away, or disappeared, we never knew what happened to them, but after that he never had problems with any kids again."

According to his report cards, he was a good student, excelling particularly in science. For the district science fair he conducted a fascinating experiment, "The Effects of Electricity on Goldfish." His biology teacher, Mr.

Cutter, wrote a note to his parents reporting, "Jack loves biology. I've never had a student show such enthusiasm about dissection. He was so excited he could hardly wait for the specimen to stop moving."

His high school yearbook *Taps* wrote that he was active in class activities, playing the title character in the senior class play, *Death Takes a Holiday* and reporting for the school newspaper the *Deadline* while serving as a volunteer for three years in the school's blood donation drive. At the school talent show he did a brilliant recitation of the Robert Frost poem "The Death of the Hired Man."

His high school sweetheart, Donna Morte, whom he dated for three years, remembers him as "a very unusual boy." Instead of giving her flowers, for example, he gave her bugs, which together they happily pressed between the pages of her diaries. "I guess we should have killed them first," she said, "but we were so in love. They messed that book up pretty good, too. I had never known how sticky bug blood was.

"I remember when he gave me a butterfly pin for my birthday. It was so beautiful. When he pinned it to my blouse, it was still flapping its wings."

At home, Jack apparently had few hobbies. Some people believe he discovered his true passion in life when he started gardening. By his own admission he had a "black thumb." Everything he planted died. His evergreens were never green. His black spruces turned dark black. Naturally, he was thrilled.

To earn extra money he took a part-time job in a pet store. Unfortunately the pet store soon went out of business, although there seems to be no record of the reason. After that he was hired by a local taxidermist where he worked as a recruiter.

He also became briefly interested in politics, doing volunteer work to raise recognition of the Endangered Species Act—although admittedly he did work for the often overlooked "pro" side.

After graduating from high school he enrolled at college in Corpus Christi, Texas. Unlike most young people, by then Jack Kevorkian was dead certain what he intended to do with his life. Eventually he enrolled in medical school, from which he proudly graduated dead last.

From there it was only a few short steps to national recognition, tremendous controversy, and finally, the special humanitarian award bestowed upon him by his favorite musical group, The Grateful Dead.

—*Nell Rogers*

An Age-Old Story

BILL GARVEY AND BETTE GLENN MET OVER A CHOCOLATE SUN-
dae in 1950 in Pasadena, California. He was a dashing
young college student and she was a beautiful waitress
at the local malt shop. It was love at first sight, and for
the next six months the two of them were inseparable.
Finally, he asked her to marry him, and they got
engaged. The wedding was to be in one year.

But there was one thing about him she just didn't
like: Bill had a terrible memory. He couldn't remember
anything: names, dates, appointments, even conversations. Bette never knew why this bothered her so
much, but for some unknown reason this one bad
habit made her furious. She knew he was a wonderful
guy with a heart of gold and this was just a small problem, but when he forgot something, it made her feel all
knotted up inside.

One night Bill forgot where he'd parked his old
jalopy and she started yelling at him. "I just can't stand
the way you forget everything." That was the begin-

ning of the big fight. Eventually she threw his ring back at him. He turned and walked away. That was the last time they saw each other for almost fifty years.

Bill went off to fight in the Korean War, and by the time he came back Bette was married and had a baby. Eventually she had three more children. Bill went to Ohio State University on the G.I. Bill and became a noted lawyer, ending up as a state court of appeals judge. He married a lovely girl he had met at Ohio State, and together they raised two kids.

In 1991 Bette's husband died. Three years later, Bill's wife also died. In 1998 Bill was visiting his brother's family in Pasadena when he went into a supermarket to pick up a few items. He was walking backward in canned goods when their baskets collided. "It's me, Bill," she said softly, "Bette Glenn." Her heart started beating rapidly.

The sky was bright with stars when he picked her up for dinner at eight that night. His hair was gray and thinner, but he was still a handsome man, she decided. And when he looked at her, he still saw a young girl smiling at him over a chocolate malt.

The night was memorable. They laughed through dinner and danced late into the evening. When he took her home, they stood on her darkened porch, close together for the first time in almost fifty years. "I can't believe it," he said, "it's like it was just yesterday."

She smiled shyly. "It was a long time ago, Billy."

"I loved you so much, Bette," he said, and leaned over to kiss her. "I've been trying to remember. What was it we broke up about?"

—*Martha McDonnell*

The Breakman:
A Grimm Christmas Fable

ONCE THERE LIVED WAY UP IN THE SKY, A LITTLE BIT NORTH OF the clouds and just west of the sunrise, the man who ran the big machine that made things break on earth. It was his responsibility to make sure that cars overheated on the hottest day of the year, that television sets quit televising just before the detective told the audience who committed the crime, and that washing machines didn't wash. Every time a computer printed, *The boy went to the fetzgqw,* he was proud. When the lights went off during a storm, or the telephone sounded as if it were underwater, or the hot water got cold just when someone was taking a shower, he knew he was doing his job.

Because he was not happy, it made him feel good to make other people unhappy. He was the kind of person who was only happy when he was unhappy. Sometimes at work he would count the number of languages in which people would yell at him for making things break. On the same day, he could start a big traffic jam in New York City and turn out all the lights in Beijing, China.

He wasn't the only breakman in the world—there were just too many things that had to be broken for one person to be able to break them all—but he was the best at what he did. He had learned that it didn't really make people angry if he broke things when they were home on Monday morning. They could just call the repairman and he would come and fix them. The best time to break things, he had learned, was on the night before a long holiday or on a Friday, when they just couldn't be fixed right away. His favorite trick of all was to break a car just before a family left on a long Christmas vacation.

Christmas came on Friday one year, which made him smile just thinking about it. That meant if he broke things on Wednesday night, it would be five whole days before people could get them fixed. He would ruin Christmas for many, many people, so he would have a very happy holiday. As the day drew closer, he made long lists of the things he would break. He was going to break cars and trains and planes, he was going to break suitcases and cameras, he was going to break bicycles and talking dolls. Oh, it was going to be a wonderful Christmas.

Finally, at six o'clock on Wednesday, he took a deep breath and turned on the big machine that broke things. The machine went *rrrr . . . oooooo . . . bump.* He pressed all the right buttons and pulled the lever again. And again the machine went *rrrr . . . oooooo . . . bump* and turned itself off. The breakman started sweating. He felt terrible—the machine that broke things was broken! He tried again and again, but it wouldn't work.

On earth, people started leaving for their vacations and there was nothing he could do about it. Angry, he tried to call the man who fixed the machine that broke things, but because it was Christmas the man wasn't working. "Call back Monday," the answering machine said.

There was nothing the breakman could do. He sat and sat and sat. He felt worse than he had ever felt in his life. He knew how much fun he was missing. And for the first time, he really understood how people on earth felt when he broke things.

On Monday, the man who repaired the machine that broke things came driving over in his big repairman truck and took out his tools and tinkered and said "Hmmm" and "Hmmm" and finally "Ahhhh," and then he said, "Okay, it's all fixed."

As soon as he heard that, the breakman felt wonderful. And he knew that this is how people on earth felt when the things that he broke got fixed. He immediately went back to his work of breaking things, but that Christmas he had learned an important lesson: no one can really be happy just by breaking things; it's also important to break the truck of the man coming to fix the things that are broken.

And the breakman lived unhappily ever after.

—*Jordan Kai Burnett*

The Greatest Commencement Speech

NO ONE EVER REMEMBERS THE COMMENCEMENT SPEAKER AT their college graduation. They're long and boring, they're full of homilies and good wishes. They rarely contain any information that might prove valuable.

At least that's what I thought when I sat down at my graduation from the University of New York City. Our speaker was the famed psychiatrist Richard H. Langsam, author of *Earn, Baby, Earn*, the controversial best-seller demonstrating how to use your anger to get rich. Langsam's speech was brief, but directly to the point, and no one in the audience that day will ever forget it.

"Ladies and gentlemen," he began, "it's a real pleasure to be here with you today. For the last four years, or for some of you, more, you have been living in a unique environment. Most of your bills were paid by your parents. You had spending money. You had the freedom to come and go as you pleased with very little responsibility. You had no boss telling you what to do or looking over your shoulder. You were surrounded by thousands of bright and attractive, and often available, single men and women. You were being exposed to some of the greatest minds in history. You got to sleep late when you wanted to. You even got the summer off and long vacations at Thanksgiving and Christmas and in midwinter.

"But now you are going out into the real world, where you'll have to earn your own money. You'll have to get up every morning and be somewhere at a specific time. You'll have to work many nights and some weekends. The responsibilities will start to grow and grow and will never stop. So I have only one question to ask you:

"What the hell is the matter with you? Why in the world would you leave here for that? Listen to me, it's really hard out there. Apparently you didn't learn anything very important here if you are willing to leave so easily. If I were sitting in your chairs, I'd make them pick me up and dump me out the door."

I was inspired by his words. The very next day I registered for graduate school. It was thanks to Richard Langsam that I eventually earned my doctorate. And then began my postgraduate work. And soon I shall begin my . . .

—*Matthew McIntosh*

Truth in Real Estate

In 1995 MEGABUILDER THOMAS ROBBINS WAS STUNNED WHEN a national poll revealed that American citizens placed little faith in the real estate industry to tell them the entire truth about properties they were considering buying. So he set out to do something about it. As a result his life has been forever changed.

Robbins had successfully built five suburban developments, which included more than seven hundred homes selling for as much as $500,000, and was just nearing completion of plans for three smaller developments when the idea struck him. One of the perks of being a builder is the opportunity to name the streets of a development. Hundreds of years ago dwellings were given names that described their location: people lived by the river or on the mountain or down in the valley or past the covered bridge. But that tradition was long forgotten by the time Robbins began building.

In his first project Robbins had named all his streets after trees, from Maple Avenue to Spruce Street—even though to build the houses he had been forced to cut down all the trees in the area. The streets of his second project were given lofty British-related names, from Devonshire Drive to Tottenham Circle, although he had never been to England. For his third development he used the names of great presidents, Lincoln Drive, Washington Avenue.

He chose those addresses, he admitted, to create an impression of status for potential buyers. They had absolutely no relation to the reality of the location. So to help rebuild faith in the real estate industry, Thomas Robbins revived the historic tradition and became the first builder in modern history to give streets names that reflected their location. Among those street names in his first development were Downwind Sewage Plant Street, Basements Flood Avenue, and Next to a Public Tennis Court Circle.

While homes on those streets did not sell well, telling this particular truth gained Robbins tremendous publicity in the industry and made him feel so good that he continued to do this in his next development. Blocks in that development included Flight Pattern Lane, Old Chemical Plant Landing, Former Swamp Road, Mosquito Haven, and Prison Overlook Drive.

While again sales were slow, Robbins bravely persisted in reviving this tradition. To see these houses potential buyers drove to the intersection of Buried Toxic Waste Street and Stagnant River View. Or they turned onto Plentiful Pollen Boulevard, Hotter 'n Hell Avenue, Bulldozed Cemetery Drive and High Taxes Court.

Robbins's efforts to promote honesty were applauded by the industry and resulted in great changes in his life.

After these houses failed to sell, Robbins's family received a court order declaring him mentally incompetent, had him institutionalized, and renamed the streets of these developments after berries, saints, and apostles, and they were quickly sold, thus ending this experiment in real estate honesty.

—*Alice Kaufman*

A Microchip Off
the Old Block

IT STARTED SO INNOCENTLY. WITH GREAT ANTICIPATION I PUR-
chased my new computer. My old computer was
almost three years old—a "dinosaur" the salesman
called it; others laughed. But it had served me well and
I felt quite comfortable with it. I'd worked countless
hours with it, we'd been through victories and defeats
together, we'd suffered through so many late nights
together, and I had actually formed a sort of emotional
bond with it.

As I took my new computer out of the box, it somehow seemed arrogant. It was shiny and sleek, it
smelled of speed, but I wondered if I would ever form a
relationship with it. We started out well. It greeted me
with a friendly "Welcome" and invited me to enter my
needs into its vaunted memory. Little did I know then
what was in its devious hard drive. Over days I discovered it was indeed as swift as promised, it whipped me
around the Internet at lightning speed, it changed
words and calculated figures and solved problems

almost instantly. Occasionally I would glance at my old computer, sitting like a cold lump, collecting dust in a corner.

I got to like my new computer. I gained confidence in its ability to supply exactly what I needed in the flash of a microchip. I saved, I downloaded; gradually I entrusted all the information of my business and personal life to it. Everything I needed daily was stored on its hard drive. I came to depend on it. And once I had made that commitment, I was powerless against it.

The first warnings came suddenly. I closed a file and with a loud chime it warned me, "Word encountered file corruption while opening c. Part of this document may be recoverable. Attempt recovery now? Yes? No?"

What? I didn't understand. Corruption? *May* be recoverable? *Attempt* recovery . . . My old computer had never threatened me like that. I wasn't sure what to do. I could feel my palms begin to sweat. Yes or no. I didn't know. Finally, I took a guess. Yes, I pressed, please yes. Do it for me. Recover what was lost.

I waited. When I again turned on the computer, everything seemed exactly as it had been. I took a deep breath. A quirk, I thought, never to be repeated.

But less than a week later with a loud *bongggg* this computer announced, "Fatal modem error . . . please close your communications applications." *Fatal?* I didn't intend to hurt anybody. Now what had I done? That seemed so . . . final. I did exactly as instructed. I raced to close everything.

Although I did not realize it at the time, this computer was now giving the orders. I hoped it would stop there.

It didn't. Three days later the next warning appeared.

"Changes have been made that affect the global template, normal. Do you want to save these changes?" Oh no! I hadn't even known I possessed a global template, yet somehow I had changed it. Global means worldwide. What had I done? What did that mean? Was this just some sort of bizarre computer joke, the kind of thing that hard drives laugh about when networking? Beads of sweat broke out on my forehead. My life was in this computer. With just a single decision I could wipe out months of work. Yes or no? I could almost hear the suspense music playing in the background. Like an actor in a movie in which the red or the blue wire has to be cut to prevent a bomb from detonating within seconds, I made a decision. I began to click on yes, then at the last second hit no. I waited.

Nothing happened. I had saved the global template. Once again my world was safe.

I no longer felt comfortable when I sat down at this computer. I recognized its power over me. And then it began threatening me, announcing suddenly, "You have performed an illegal operation!" Me? No, I hadn't. Yes, I had, it coldly insisted. But it refused to tell me what it was—or what the penalty might be. In my whole life, with the exception of going through yellow traffic lights and gleefully tearing warnings off mattresses, I had never performed an illegal operation in my life. In my mind I saw a vision of a doctor leaning over a patient . . . but that wasn't me. I didn't know what to do, where to turn. Who else knew about this?

I sat perfectly still, not knowing what to do. Somewhere, I suspected, a programmer was laughing diabolically. I realized I had no choice, I had to get out of this situation. Gently, I moved my cursor to the box that asked "OK?" Okay? I had to laugh at that. No, it wasn't okay. I hit the mouse once, twice, and waited.

I couldn't believe what I had gotten myself into. Corruption. Fatalities. Illegal operations. I had become a one-man crime ring.

So here I sit in front of this computer, knowing full well that it's just a machine, a device to simplify my life, a servant—and yet I know this computer has the ability to destroy me with just the switch of a microchip. And just as with my old computer, we have formed a relationship. But in this case I do everything it tells me to do: I shut off applications at its command, I stop performing illegal operations, I wait when it says wait.

In the corner my old friend still sits, dead now, but sometimes I think I see it monitoring the situation. And smiling.

—Taylor Jesse Stevens

The Ultimate Fat-Free, Low-Cholesterol, Low-Sodium Diet

At one time or another most women have looked enviously at glamorous photographs of supermodels and wondered, why can't I look like that? We've all heard it: I'd kill to look like that even just for one day. Well, the fact is anyone can! Introducing the ultimate diet: fat free, low cholesterol, low sodium—and absolutely guaranteed to make those pounds just melt away.

This amazing diet was discovered thousands of years ago and has been proven to work through the annals of recorded history. It worked for the ancient Egyptians and will work for you! Even modern science has yet to find a more effective weight-loss program. And unlike other diet plans there are no costly food supplements or substitutes to purchase, no pills to take several times a day, no expensive books to buy. There are no complicated recipes to follow, no color-coded tickets, no visits to a medical professional.

You choose the amount of weight you want to lose—and then do it. No frills, no fries, no fat. By following this diet for only three months—sometimes even sooner—it is possible to lose your entire body weight! It's simple to follow and easy to remember. Here, then, the diet of the supermodels:

Daily Allowance

	Amount per Serving
Calories	0
Calories from fat	0
Total fat	0
Saturated fat	0
Polyunsaturated fat	0
Monounsaturated fat	0
Cholesterol	0
Sodium	0
Potassium	0
Vitamin A	0
Vitamin C	0
Calcium	0
Iron	0
Vitamin D	0
Thiamin	0
Riboflavin	0
Niacin	0
Vitamin B_6	0
Folic Acid	0
Vitamin B_{12}	0
Phosphorus	0
Magnesium	0
Zinc	0

—*Robert Fielding*

A "Poor" Movie

WHEN DIRECTOR JONATHON BOSWELL SET OUT TO MAKE A movie about poverty in America today, he did not realize how difficult that would be. Initially all the major studios rejected his proposal, fearing that moviegoers would not be willing to spend an average of $7.50 a ticket to watch a film about poor people. Only after Academy Award-winning actors Michael Garvey and Maureen Jahan agreed to work for half their normal $20 million fee was it possible for Boswell to find financing for his stirring film *Forget Us Not*.

"This was a film I had to make," Boswell explains. "I remember the first time I saw *Grapes of Wrath* [and] what it did to me. And then the CBS documentary *Harvest of Shame* just tore me up inside. I wanted to do a modern version of that old story. I was determined to remind people that even in the midst of this great economic boom that there still are some people without their own 401K's to fall back on, that there still are some people who haven't founded their own Internet companies, that there are people out there struggling to make payments on their second car, people who have to struggle through life on only two television sets. When we began researching this film, I was stunned to discover that there are thousands of children out there who have never even heard the word Nintendo!"

When production began, the original budget of under $10 million quickly spiraled. "I didn't want to do the so-called Hollywood version of poverty," Boswell continued, as he sat in his hotel room in New York's Sherry Netherland Hotel, overlooking Central Park. "I wanted the audience to really know what it feels like when it's five degrees above zero outside and you don't even have a safe, warm island in the Caribbean to go to, or not to know what restaurant you're next meal is coming from. I wanted the audience to experience real poverty in this country. I wanted them to go into those big theaters and sit in those stadium seats and be really uncomfortable."

The film, which critics have hailed as "a masterpiece of despair," eventually cost more than $70 million to make. "As we discovered, poverty is not cheap," Boswell continued. "I had to fight the studio for every penny. Our costume budget alone was more than a million dollars. We had to hire one of the expensive diet doctors in America to watch our actors during filming to make sure they remained healthy. We had originally intended to shoot on location, but we just couldn't get the mood we needed. So we ended up building our own set on a backlot.

"It was an incredible set. When we brought our technical advisers over to see it, and these were actual poor people we found on the streets of Beverly Hills, I mean they were practically crying it was so lifelike."

But the key to the success of the film, Boswell believes, was the dedication of his stars. "Look, this was not an easy role for Mike Garvey to play. For his entire career he's played handsome, leading men. But he was absolutely committed to this performance. I mean, he fired his driver and actually drove himself to work in his landscaper's ten-year-old Honda. And on the set he stayed completely in character. I mean, he was always trying to borrow money from members of the crew.

"And Dolly Berkow's performance, I think, gives new meaning to the word *poor*. I can't recall another actress acting as poorly as she does."

Perhaps the biggest surprise to Boswell has been the unexpected success of the product tie-ins campaign. Many companies that declined to be involved with the picture felt the theme did not lend itself to merchandising. But The Ole Cabin chain of Southern-style fast-food restaurants has had great success with its po'boy two-for-one promotion, and the action figures have also done well. The impact of the film has also been felt in beauty parlors throughout the country, as women have demanded that hairstylists duplicate Jahan's free-flowing yet structured look created especially for this film by legendary stylist Ted Feurey.

The sound-track album, consisting of music written especially for the film by D'lars&Sense, immediately shot to the top of the charts. In honor of the picture's theme the group donated a percentage of the profits from the CD to its favorite charity, The D'lars&Sense Foundation.

But most rewarding to Boswell has been the attention given to the problem of poverty in America. "Hollywood is often criticized for being out of touch with real issues facing this country. I think with this film we can change that impression."

The good news for stockholders in the studio is that this look at poverty in America has proven a box office bonanza—the stock has gained eighty-one cents a share on receipts.

—*Shane Tyler Ehrman*

My Roommate

I'LL NEVER FORGET THE DAY THE LETTER CAME FROM THE UNIVERsity telling me the name of my freshman roommate. My heart sank as I read this letter. I could tell just from her name and hometown that she was different from me. I wanted a roommate just like me, someone who could be my friend. "I just know I'll hate her," I cried to my mother.

"Oh, I'm sure she'll be just fine," my mother said, dismissing my fears. "I'm sure she's a lovely girl."

"No," I insisted, "I'll bet she's really a weirdo." I'd always heard these great stories of roommates becoming lifelong friends. That's what I wanted. But in my mind I could just imagine what she looked like. This was the universe bouncing my karma back to me, I decided, giving me as a roommate exactly the kind of person my friends and I had always made fun of. "Oh, I can't believe I have to room with someone with a name like that," I said sadly.

"Oh, come on, it's only for the first semester," my mother said. "After that you can always change."

That letter practically ruined the rest of my summer. I dreaded meeting her. Three months later I left for college with great trepidation. I got there a day before she did and I was sitting on my bed when the door opened and she walked in lugging one large suitcase. At first, in the dim lights I couldn't see her very well, but when she walked toward me and I finally got a good look at her, I was shocked. She had a little diamond nose ring and two lip rings.

I couldn't believe this was actually happening. "Wow," I said, "those are beautiful!"

"Thanks," she said, and when she opened her mouth, I saw she also had a tongue ring! She was dressed in all black; her hair was black and clipped really short. She looked fabulous. "Hey, could you give me a hand with my voodoo altar? It's pretty big."

I couldn't believe it. She had brought her own sacrificial altar! And it was even bigger than mine. I knew we were going to be the only people in the whole dorm with *two* altars.

I began helping her unpack. "Why don't you put on some music," she suggested. When I opened her CD carrying case, I almost felt like crying. She had all the groups I loved: Death to All Capitalists, Splinters under Your Fingernails, Code Blue, even the new Pain Makers. This seemed too good to be true. I put on a Nihilist album and turned the volume way up as we began putting away her things.

I could see she was trying to tell me something, but I couldn't hear her. *"What?"* I shouted in her ear.

"Make it louder!" she shouted right back.

I nodded my head. Later, after we'd finished and we were lying down, she started telling me about herself. "You got a boyfriend?" I asked.

She laughed at that. "Men are disgusting. They're superficial and I only exploit them when I need something."

I just couldn't believe we had so much in common. Later that night we compared tattoos; we even had similiar Iron Crosses on our ankles. And she smoked the same brand of Turkish cigarettes I did. It was amazing. Only a few short hours earlier I was afraid that my roomie was going to be really weird. I could not have been more wrong. When I finally called home that night, my mother wanted to know all about her. "She's great, Mom," I said, "she hates all the same things I do!

"You were right. I've learned never to judge anyone before you meet them."

And that was a lesson I've never forgotten.

—*Emily Rachael Perschetz*

My Village

In these demanding days, stated Hillary Rodham Clinton, it requires the contribution of many people to raise a child. It takes a village, she said. When I read those words, I thought it might be me she was writing about. It took a lot of people to help me get to where I am today. Like so many kids, my parents fought often and loudly and finally got divorced. I lived with my mother, who worked full-time at a company that made prosthetic devices for animals, so each afternoon I came home from school to an empty apartment. I became a latchkey kid.

The first person to have a significant influence on my life beyond my parents was my sixth-grade teacher, Miss Farber. I wasn't a good student at all; a lot of people told me I wasn't trying hard enough, but I knew they were wrong. I was just smart enough to know that I really wasn't very smart. It was Miss Farber who told me, "If you're not going to work hard, you're just wasting your time and my time in school, young man.

If you don't want to use that noodle of yours, why do you even bother to come to school?"

She made a lot of sense to me. So I stopped going to school. The next person who influenced me was a security guard at the Post Road Mall, Mr. T. L. Jones. It was Mr. Jones who first grabbed me for shoplifting. It wasn't very much, I just put three sweaters on under my shirt and tried to walk out, but he stopped me. As this was the first time I had ever been caught, Mr. Jones had the option of releasing me with a warning. But he knew the value of punishment, so he handed me over to the police.

It was then I met Officer Frank Wyman. Frank Wyman was a special kind of policeman, and over the next few years we spent a lot of time together. Officer Wyman got to know me well, so whenever I went to the mall, he would follow me. It was Officer Wyman who arrested me four different times for theft.

I know my life would have been very different if I'd never met Judge Gibson. Judge Gibson believed there was no such thing as a bad kid—that a bad kid was just a miniature bad adult. So although I was barely eighteen, he sentenced me to eighteen months in prison.

In prison I met Mike "Lefty" Brown. Lefty and I became cellmates and best friends, and I learned so much from him. It was Lefty who convinced me that I had been wasting my life stealing from malls. "That's a sucker bet," he told me, "the real money is in cars." Lefty taught me everything he knew about stealing cars, and when I was released, he even introduced me to people who helped me get started in the business. Eventually I graduated to burglary and suburban-house robberies.

Today I am one of the most successful thieves in this

country. It took the efforts of a lot of people to help me get to this point. Without my parents, my teacher, the security guard, policeman, judge, and cellmate, I could not possibly have reached this position. To them I remain eternally grateful. And who knows, maybe someday I'll prove Hillary Clinton was correct: while I have never taken a whole village, I have robbed five houses on the same block. But I do like her concept.

—*Michael Norman*

The Modern Bible

WHEN I WAS A CHILD, I READ THE BIBLE FROM COVER TO cover in Sunday school. I could repeat all of the wonderful stories it told. But as I grew older, got married, and had a family of my own, I rarely had time to revisit this old friend. Besides, I thought, I had already learned all the important lessons.

But recently, while I was in a hotel room on a business trip I opened a drawer and inside was a brand-new Bible. It was a new edition titled "A Bible for Our Time." I picked up this trusted friend—and as I leafed through the once familiar pages, I felt as if I had never read this book before. It was as if I were reading it through entirely new eyes. For this time I brought with me the wisdom of experience.

I remembered reading long ago the incredible story of Moses leading the Israelites out of Egypt. But as I read it once again these many years later, I found it was very different from what I remembered. What had once seemed to be a tale of great faith rewarded suddenly took on an entirely new meaning. In this story the Israelites had fled from Egypt, only to be pursued by the armies of the evil pharaoh. Upon reaching the Red Sea, which seemed to block their passage, Moses appealed to the Lord for help. "Let the waters be parted," he beseeched.

The Lord heard the prayers of this good man, and in response the Red Sea separated. Moses and the Israelites walked across to the Promised Land. But when the pharaoh's armies tried to follow, the ocean closed in on them, engulfing the soldiers. The Israelites were saved.

Once I had believed that to be the end of that story. As I discovered though, there was much more to it. After resting from the long journey, Moses found himself in desperate need of a cleansing. Upon finding a small stream in which to bathe, he stripped himself bare and walked into the cooling waters.

And just like the great Red Sea, the water in this stream also separated. Moses walked right into the middle of it without even getting damp. While this was confusing, Moses said nothing, for Moses was not a complainer.

The next day it rained. Rain, Moses knew, was the Lord's gift to the land. The rain poured down, and Moses thanked the Lord for this. But again, as Moses stepped from his shelter, the rain separated around him as if he were standing under the leaves of a great tree. He moved through the storm untouched by even the smallest drop.

By now several weeks had sped by without Moses feeling the coolness of water. And the Israelites could know when Moses walked among them from the scent of his labors and other things. The Israelites gathered water in the bowls they had carried through the desert and endeavored to spill upon Moses these waters, but to no avail. Just as the sea had moved away from him, so did all water.

And now even when Moses was standing many hectares away from his people, when the wind blew right, it was as if he were standing right next to them. So they moved farther away from him. And then farther. Even the perfume of the great olive tree was no longer enough to mask the coming of Moses. Small children and the sheep fled from him.

So it came to be known that wherever Moses went there was no water nearby. Thus, for the next forty years Moses wandered in the desert, searching for water.

As I put down that great book that night, I realized with amazement that even after so many years I was once again learning new and important lessons from it. For that night I had learned, as had Moses, *Be really careful what you wish for, because you might just get it.*

—*Alex Langsam*

The Incredible Journey of Little Tiger

EVERY ONCE IN A WHILE A HUMAN-INTEREST STORY CAPTURES
the attention of the American public. For six weeks
during the summer of 1991 millions of people across
the nation followed the incredible saga of the grit, loyalty and determination of a tiny dog reporters named
the Little Tiger. Tiger wasn't much of any kind of special breed; they referred to him as a "Heinz," meaning
he was fifty-seven varieties of dog. He was nothing
more than a mutt, but his journey showed millions of
people the real meaning of love.

No one knew where he had come from when he was
first discovered walking along Route 17 in New Jersey.
A reporter for the *Newark News*, George Cole, picked
him up and took him home. The dog was hungry and
dirty, making it obvious he had been on the road for
some time. He was wearing a collar, but the identifica-
tion tag had broken off. He was a gentle dog, terrific
with Cole's young children. Cole knew that somewhere there was a family desperately missing this dog.

For three days he tried unsuccessfully to find out where the dog might have come from.

The dog desperately missed his owner. Day and night he sat by the door whining to be released. He had a journey to make and he wanted to get started. Finally Cole decided to let the dog take this dangerous trip. The day he opened the door and let the dog go, he wrote a column asking people to watch out for this sweet animal and, if they spotted him, to call him with reports of the dog's progress. That was the beginning of this incredible tale of loyalty and perseverance.

Two days after releasing the dog Cole received the first report. The dog was walking west, seemingly knowing exactly where he was going. The Associated Press picked up the story and it ran nationwide—and suddenly this little dog became a celebrity. Hugh Downs did a segment about this dog on the television program *20/20,* and people all across the country began following this trip step by step. By the time he reached Missouri, the AP was issuing hourly reports. Reporters from other nations picked up the story, and countless millions around the world joined Americans in opening their hearts to this little dog with a mission. People put out food for him, and he would pause for a few bites, but no one tried to stop him.

It was a tough journey. The dog, dubbed Little Tiger by a journalist because of his determination, walked through day and night, rain and snow. In Kansas he walked through a blinding snowstorm. In Nebraska temperatures below zero didn't even slow him down. He was going to get back to his family no matter what it took.

There were many close calls. In Utah he barely

escaped death when an eighteen-wheeler almost ran him over. In Colorado a pit bull chased him, but he managed to get safely away. Little Tiger was obviously a smart dog; facing the Rocky Mountains, he jumped into the back of a pickup truck and hitched a ride through the mountains.

Behind this remarkable journey lay a mystery that intrigued millions of people. How had he been separated from his owners? Who were they and where were they? And with all this publicity, surely they must have been aware of his plight and yet they did not step forward.

From time to time people walked alongside him for miles, but he seemed not to notice. He just kept walking, sure of his destination. The only thing that slowed him was a stray female spaniel he met in Utah that captured his fancy. The two dogs played happily for hours, but then, after giving her a last loving lick, Little Tiger continued on his quest.

The last few days of this walk were covered live by CNN. Every half hour the network would switch to a mobile crew following the dog for the latest update. Little Tiger walked through the city of Laguna Niguel, California, trailed now, as he was obviously headed toward the end of his journey, by hundreds of people either walking or following in a three-mile-long car caravan. He walked into the town, past a large mall, down a small street, his pace quickening. He was going home.

Finally, six weeks after he began this journey, he ran up the steps of a small, lovely house and started barking loudly, leaping into the air. He was home, he was home. The front door opened and a man in his late thirties stared out to see camera crews and hundreds of people standing there as the police department hurried to put up barriers.

The man stared at the huge crowd in disbelief from inside the house where he had been hidden by the Witness Protection Program. Little Tiger's real name, it turned out, was Bozo the dog, and his owner, John Reynolds, was better known as Johnny the Rat. The little dog had been left behind three months earlier when Reynolds and his family were suddenly moved in the middle of the night after his testimony had put dozens of members of organized crime and corrupt union officials in prison.

Reynolds had been scheduled to testify in many trials, and apparently the mob had been searching desperately for him. Two months later Reynolds went out for a slice of pizza and was never seen again.

—*Katie Robbins*

The Lucky Winner

It is better to have loved and lost than just to have bet and lost.
—BART REICH

KATHY GLENN HAS HER BELOVED DOG TO THANK FOR WINNING $8.75 million in the New York State Lottery. Lucky Kathy had forgotten to buy food for her hungry eleven-year-old terrier, Pal, who was whining insistently. So Kathy, who would otherwise have stayed home for the evening, drove to a local store and bought dog food—and with the change bought a single lottery ticket. Three hours later she was a multimillionaire.

Beating the 43 million-to-1 odds, the winner had been playing the lottery irregularly for six years, always using the same numbers: 9, 14, 24, 31, 35, 40. How did the lucky winner pick those numbers?

Each of them has a special meaning to her:

Nine was her age when her mother and father left her in front of the orphanage and drove away, never to be seen again.

Fourteen was the number of operations she had after an out-of-control taxicab careened through the front of a restaurant causing the accident in which she lost her left arm.

6 1

Twenty-four was her age when she first contracted the rare disease that causes her to suddenly and for no apparent reason begin squawking like a duck.

Thirty-one was her age when the house she'd bought with her insurance money from the cab was accidentally destroyed by the first tornado reported in upstate New York in more than one hundred years.

Thirty-five was the number of years the accountant who was handling what remained of her money was sentenced to after stealing it and investing in Remington Typewriter futures.

Forty was the number of times she called the police to respond to a domestic disturbance during her brief marriage.

The lucky Ms. Glenn has chosen to receive the money in annual payments rather than one lump sum. Ironically, she was so excited to learn she'd won, she left the door open and the dog that had made it all possible ran outside and was hit by a car.

—*Risa Schlow*

My First Date

I DON'T KNOW WHO WAS MORE NERVOUS BEFORE MY FIRST real date, my father or me. I was sixteen years old and this was the first time a boy was taking me out to a movie and dinner. I'm sure it was difficult for my father, I'd been his Little Princess for so long that it was hard for him to see me grow up. He had always been so protective of me, watching out for me, taking care of me. I was terrified that he would think no boy was good enough for his daughter.

When Danny rang the bell, I invited him in to meet my father and mother. Truthfully, I had been dreading this moment for several years. "Nice to meet you, Danny," my father said, shaking hands with him. "There's just a few little things I'd like to ask you."

I'm sure my face turned redder than a ripe tomato, but Danny handled it well. "Sure, sir, go right ahead."

Sir? The moment Danny called my father "Sir," I took a deep breath. My father had been a career military man, a gruff staff sergeant, and I knew he loved

6 3

that Danny respected him. My father asked all the proper questions: Where were we going? Who were we going with? "Who's driving?"

"I am, sir. I have my license and I've worked every summer to be able to buy my car. I had it checked yesterday by an excellent mechanic, who assures me nothing will go wrong. I've got a full tank of gas and even plenty of oil. Don't worry, sir, your daughter will be safe with me."

"You're not going to have anything to drink?"

"Oh, no, of course not. I don't drink."

"What time will you be home?"

"By twelve-thirty on the dot." Danny was amazing, he had the right answer for every question my father asked. I'm not sure my father liked that. Knowing him, I was afraid he might think Danny was too confident.

"Just a couple more questions," my father continued. "Suppose terrorists stop your car and kidnap my daughter, put her in a steel box, and bury her three feet below the ground. What would you do?"

"I'd feign unconsciousness. Then after getting their license plate number, I'd follow them in my own car. If my car didn't work, I'd commandeer a vehicle. After notifying the police, I'd watch from a distance until they left. Then I would use the hammer and nails I always carry to make holes in the box to ensure she had plenty of air. Then I would dig up the box and let her out, and we would still be home by twelve-thirty."

I could see my father was impressed. "All right, now suppose you're in the movie theater and a fire breaks out. The ushers have locked all the exit doors to prevent people from sneaking in, so you can't use them and the crowd is blocking the aisles—"

"Dad, please," I interrupted, "you're embarrassing me."

"I'm sorry, honey, but I worry about you." He returned to his question. "The theater is getting very smoky and you can't see. What are you going to do?"

"I'd start by putting my jacket over her head, being careful not to muss her hair. Then I would lead her to the back, avoiding the aisles and stepping over the seats. When we reached the rear of the theater, I would take her into a rest room because I've already checked and they have windows leading to an alley. I would break the window and help your daughter climb out. Then we would immediately call you to tell you we were all right."

"I see," my father said, then asked, "Men's room or ladies' room?"

"Men's room, sir. But her head would be covered with my jacket so she wouldn't be exposed to anything unseemly."

I was starting to get upset. "Dad, the movie's going to start."

"Sweetheart, I've just met Danny, and while he seems like a fine young man, I just want to ask him a few simple questions." He pointed at Danny. "Okay, a commando squad from a foreign nation has surrounded the diner and taken everyone inside hostage. They're threatening to start killing hostages if their countrymen are not released. The police have been called but they can't do anything. You're inside and one of the commandos seems to be interested in my daughter. Just what are you going to do about it?" By the time my father finished, he was standing toe-to-toe with Danny, screaming in his face.

"Well, in that case," Danny responded, "I guess I'd have to use a little jujitsu." With that, he picked up my father and flipped him over his right shoulder, sending him flying right into the couch.

My mother had been watching the whole thing. She got terribly upset. "Dear," she said to my father, "stop playing. Someone's going to get hurt."

Danny helped my father get up. My father seemed pleased with that answer. He was breathing heavily. "Then one of them takes out a pistol," he said, reaching under his shirt to pull out a pistol, which he pointed at Danny. "How you going to get out of there?"

"I guess I have to go for the heavy artillery," Danny said, pulling out the biggest gun I'd ever seen from his sports jacket. "I shoot a few of them to create a diversion, then lead her into the kitchen. I'd throw her in a metal laundry cart and start pushing it out at full speed. At the last possible moment I'd dive in and cover her body with my own body, being careful not to touch her in any inappropriate place. As soon as we got free, I would drive her right home because I know you'd be worried about her."

Danny was still standing there holding the gun. I didn't know what to say. This was the most incredibly embarrassing moment of my life—Danny's gun was bigger than my father's! "Daddy, please, can we go now?"

"Sure," he said, smiling and putting his gun back in his belt. "You kids run along. Have a good time." He stood at the door watching until we drove away, knowing a part of our lives had ended. That was a long time ago, but as long as I live, I will never forget how he worried about his Little Princess.

—*Marsha Perkins*

The Bottle of Champagne

MY FATHER'S CLOSEST FRIEND GAVE HIM A LOVELY BOTTLE OF champagne on the day I was born. My father put this bottle of champagne in the refrigerator to await the perfect day to open it. Birthdays and anniversaries came and went and still my father refused to open this bottle of champagne. "When will you open it?" I asked as I got older.

"Someday," he said, "but it has to be a very special day."

Years went by and still he refused to open it. Many people knew about the bottle of champagne in the refrigerator and asked my father when he intended to open it. At the right time, he kept telling them.

Through those years the bottle of champagne grew in importance. If he refused to open it for my sixteenth birthday or my parents' twentieth anniversary, that meant that the event for which he did open it had to be more important than everything that had preceded it. As he got older, people asked about it more and more often. When? I don't know, he replied. But when?

When my brother married, my father took it out of the refrigerator—then put it back. When his first grandchild was born, he put his hand on the cork, then stopped. Not yet, he said, not yet.

The bottle of champagne had become an obsession with him. He carried it with him to every major family event. At night, my mother said, he sometimes just stared at it. For that bottle had become symbolic of his whole life. For him, nothing seemed important enough to open it. He was still waiting for something he could not identify to happen.

But finally, one day he announced to everyone that he would be opening the bottle of champagne the following Tuesday. Not to celebrate a single event, he explained, but rather to acknowledge his satisfaction with his entire life.

And once he announced that decision, I could see the change sweep over him. Relieved of that responsibility, he relaxed. No one would ever again ask him when he was going to open the bottle of champagne.

That Tuesday the entire family and many of my father's friends came to the house—among them the man who had originally given him the bottle of champagne. And just before my father opened the bottle, this good friend quieted the crowd and told them, "I am very pleased to be here today, as our beloved friend finally opens this bottle. We've all waited a long time for this. And so, to honor this very special day, I have brought him this bottle of champagne . . ."

—*Mack Kelly*

The Powers of the Pokémon

I, TOO, ONCE WAS A NONBELIEVER. I, TOO, ONCE BELIEVED that Pokémon were fictional characters whose powers were about as real as those magazine ads announcing I'd won the sweepstakes. Having grown up with Superman and Batman and Spiderman, I had learned long ago that these were nothing more than artistic creations. While it had been fun to believe in their existence, the reality was that no man or woman had any extraordinary powers.

By the time I became the parent of two young children, I had also lived through the garbage pail kids, Cabbage Patch Kids dolls, *Star Wars,* Power Rangers, the Spice Girls, the *Toy Story* gang, even Barney. While admittedly I thought most of these fads were sort of silly, I also accepted that kids enjoyed them. But no one believed they really existed; the Cabbage Patch Kids dolls weren't really born, the Power Rangers weapons didn't really fire, the Spice Girls couldn't really sing. So when I first learned about the Pokémon I assumed this was simply the next new fad, the latest attempt to capture the hearts—and allowances—of America's children.

Each type of Pokémon, I learned, supposedly had different powers and different strengths. There were 151 different types, and they could be captured and controlled by "trainers." Cute, I thought, but no different from all the other children's superheroes. When my children tried to tell me their powers were real, I smiled and agreed with them, but I knew the truth.

Or so I thought.

I remember the night I began to suspect that perhaps there was more to these funny little characters than I had previously believed. It was a typical school night— I was fighting to get the kids into bed. I screamed, I yelled, I threatened, but against a ten-year-old and an eight-year-old I was powerless. And then, out of desperation, I said the magic words: "If you get into bed right now, I'll buy you each a pack of Pokémon cards."

Within seconds the Pokémon had accomplished what I had failed to do in an hour! It was an awesome display of power.

I dismissed it almost immediately. These things weren't real, I knew, so they couldn't have any real powers. Yet the very next day it happened again. Eat! I begged my kids. Please eat! But we don't like food, they responded for perhaps the millionth time. In my desperation I reached to the depths of my belief system—I invoked the spirit of the Pokémon: "If you eat everything on your plate, I'll take you to the fast-food place for Pokémon balls!"

Never before had I seen anything quite so amazing. There was no whizzing of a red cape or bat signal in the sky or flash of green light, but almost instantly both children had cleaned their plates.

No, I thought to myself, it can't be. These are mythical creatures, they can't possibly have real powers. Yet the evidence was growing they were far more powerful than any parent.

The next night I put their powers to an even greater test: not for a moment did I really believe that the Pokémon were powerful enough to . . . make my children take a bath! I applied a strict scientific method. At first I tried myself. I used all the tricks I'd learned and then resorted to the usual threats. All to no avail. Only when I was certain that I had exhausted my own powers did I dare once again invoke the powers of the Pokémon: "First one in the tub gets a Pokémon pencil sharpener!"

Within seconds I was convinced. I had seen something I had never before seen: two children arguing over who got to take a bath first!

I fell to my knees in reverence. I believe! I cried out. I believe! Since that time I have come to accept completely the superpowers of the Pokémon. I have seen the Pokémon make children happily do their homework, go to a relative's house, be home on time, stop hitting their sibling, even offer to walk the dog—and we don't even have a dog.

I believed so strongly that I was surprised to learn that many principals prohibited students from bringing their Pokémon cards to school. I wondered, are these people out of their mind? Teachers have as many as thirty children in a single classroom. Only the awesome powers of a Pokémon could make these children unite and listen to their teacher. If only teachers knew,

I thought, that the powers of the creatures are real. If they only knew that the Pokémon have more strength than a hundred parents to move a seven-year-old! Educational miracles could be accomplished simply by saying the magic words. "The next person who speaks gets their Pokémon cards taken away."

I have seen the light—and it is shining brightly on new Pokémon cards.

But, I fear, like Superman when exposed to Kryptonite, these powers have limits yet undiscovered. For recently I felt a chill running down my spine when I asked one of the kids where his Pokémon cards were and he responded, "I don't know. I think I left them somewhere," and walked away.

—*David Malinsky*

The Shape of Advertising

Let sleeping politicians lie.
—Confusion

I WAS SITTING IN THE BACK OF THE LARGE LECTURE HALL WHEN
the old man shuffled slowly to the podium. The room
was crowded, people were standing in the back, but no
one made a sound. We were there to see and hear a
legend, William "Bill" Madden, considered by many to
be the father of modern advertising. It was well known
that he was quite sick and this might be his final public
appearance.

"I'm an advertising man," he began in a soft voice that
grew stronger as he spoke, "and damn proud of it. While
some foolish people may dismiss advertising as nothing
more than an expensive way to sell, it's a lot more than
that. I think it is fair to say that advertising has shaped
our culture. It has helped define who we are as a society.

"When I began my career in advertising more than half
a century ago, it was a different ball game. We just sat
down and did it, stumbling our way through the days. We
had never even heard the word *demo*"—he paused to
emphasize it here—"*graphics*. But my, how that has

changed. In these busy days the competition for the eyes of the consumer is extreme. Advertising has become a complex science. We'll try anything to reach the people we want to reach. Now we use surveys and focus groups, test campaigns, rollout marketing, polls and in-depth interviewing. We use every conceivable type of media, and when they invent a new way to communicate we'll use that too.

"And what we've learned is that effective advertising is the result of great research. It begins with pinpointing the exact needs and desires of the person you are trying to reach, and creating the kind of advertising that will appeal directly to your target audience.

"Once we actually believed you could advertise to every segment of the population the same way. We sure know differently now. Basically, all advertising can be broken down into three general areas: consumer products, business products, and service advertising. Each is very different and each requires an entirely different approach.

"Let's look at consumer advertising, everything from cereal and clothes to computers and cars. The industry has dissected this market a thousand ways. We've sliced it and diced it and then broken it down by age and gender, income, location, areas of interest . . . you name it, we can give you the statistics. We have gathered so much information about our customer we could make a pretty good prediction about what kind of socks he'd be wearing on a rainy Tuesday in March. It cost a fortune to gather this information, a fortune. And after analyzing every megabyte of data on our specially developed computer databases, we learned that the best way to capture the attention of this segment of the advertising universe is to use a pretty young girl wearing sexy clothing driving a fancy car.

"Of course, selling to people in business is totally different. Totally. This is everything from copiers to renting entire buildings. The business customer today is very sophisticated. This customer is attuned to price differential, quality, location, even support. How do you gain this customer's undivided attention? It's not easy, these people are busy running a business. They lack the leisure time that consumers have. Getting the attention of the business customer is much more difficult than attracting a consumer, so according to every measurement we can take, the best way to reach the business customer is to use *two* pretty girls wearing sexy clothing driving a fancy car.

"The service market, once again, requires a unique marketing strategy. Selling services is entirely different from selling package goods or hard goods. The single most important aspect of selling service, ladies and gentlemen, whether it be health care or housepainting, is trust. In the service business, trust is everything. The task is to convince the consumer to trust your client as opposed to the competition. Numerous studies have shown three ingredients are necessary to do this: testimonials from previous customers, strong financial guarantees of quality, and perhaps most important of all, as many pretty girls as possible wearing sexy clothing driving a fancy car.

"Now, those are the secrets of great advertising."

We stood up as one and roared as the old man walked quietly to his seat, knowing we would never forget the wisdom of his words. For in his few brief remarks, he had made crystal clear the great shape of advertising in America!

—*Franklyn Biondo*

My Old Clunker

I'LL NEVER FORGET THE DAY I DROVE THAT CAR OUT OF THE showroom and proudly parked it right in front of my house. I'd been saving for this car a long time, ever since I first saw her picture in an ad in *Life* magazine. She sparkled brightly in the sunlight, like a dream come true. The chrome bumpers reflected my image, the hood ornament shined, and the whitewall tires glistened with the promise of the miles to come.

And best of all was the smell of her brand-new real leather seats. Sometimes at night those first few weeks, when the kids were asleep and Marge was doing the dishes, I'd sneak out to the driveway and just sit there, inhaling deeply that scent. There is nothing like the aroma of a new car. For the first few weeks, every Saturday afternoon I'd wash and wax the car. I loved that car so much I held my breath when I put the kids in the backseat and took them for a ride.

That was many years and 112,000 miles ago. Now the old clunker is about ready for the junkyard. Her outside is faded and scratched, her tires are just about bald, and some of the lights are cracked. Inside the seats are torn, the radio and the speedometer long ago stopped working, and the floor is littered with everything from gum wrappers to empty bottles.

But I don't see those things when I look at her. Instead I see the memories of a growing family. When I look at the backseat, I can still smell the first time six-year-old Danny got carsick. Oh, sure, maybe it was our fault, maybe we shouldn't have let him have three hamburgers with onions and ketchup and grape juice before that trip, but we were so young. Maybe I did overreact a little; I guess I shouldn't have kept Danny locked in the trunk for *two* whole days—but this was the first new car I'd ever owned.

At first I didn't even want to dirty the ashtray, and I kept the floor immaculate. But the reality is that after you drop the first empty beer bottle on the floor, it becomes easier and easier to let the residue of daily living pile up. After a while, in fact, I found the familiar clink of empty beer bottles rattling around reassuring.

For a long time I even kept her glove compartment neat. I had the warranty book and the repair manual and the little tool kit that came with the car in there and nothing else. But gradually I started putting other things in there, things like the receipts for gas and repairs, threats from the collection agency, notes from my parole officer, even warnings from Marge's divorce lawyer. After a while it got so stuffed there was hardly even enough room for my gun and ammunition.

She's wearing her third set of tires now and the treads are just about worn-out. I can remember running my hands over her first tires, how firm and thick that rubber felt. Those treads were so deep I had real difficulty cleaning them after I ran over the old cat. But by the time I hit that dog, the treads were well worn and it was much easier to clean the tires.

I remember each night walking around the outside of the car to make sure I hadn't gotten even a scratch in that beautiful paint job. If you truly love a car, you never forget that first nick. I know that person in the parking lot who carelessly opened his door and scratched mine certainly never will. I guess I gave him something to remember it by, me and my close friend Mr. Crowbar. I'll bet he had a nice cool ride home without that front windshield.

There's a big difference between a small scratch and a big dent. I loved that car and did everything possible to protect it. But other drivers weren't as careful. I will never forget that first dent. I was on the highway when a driver cut in front of me without looking. We almost had a bad accident. That was so dangerous that to protect other people I felt I had to show him what could have happened. Actually, that's where the first four or five dents came from. But I knew that driver would never cut in front of anyone else again—at least not in the car he was driving.

As I drove that old car to the junkyard, all these memories came rushing back to me. All the laughs and tears and cries and whines and screams, all the shouting and arguing. I remember that wonderful new-car smell and then the overwhelming scent of perfume that filled the air—and I remember how upset my wife was when she also smelled it. But now, when I inhale deeply, I can still detect that unmistakable aroma of formaldehyde coming from the trunk.

It's been a long time since my wife and I bought that old car, and as I watch that enormous compactor press it into a tiny square of metal, I know that I will really miss her.

And, of course, I'll miss the old car too.

—*George Hicker*

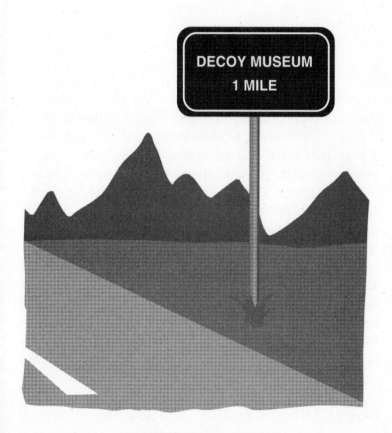

ACTUAL ROAD SIGN

The Times of Your Life

HAVE YOU EVER WONDERED WHERE YOUR TIME GOES? WELL, if you're the average person, you spend about 15 hours a year, that's two and a half minutes per day, brushing your teeth. But you also spend slightly more than 106 days fast asleep. Those are only some of the surprising statistics contained in a recently issued report on time management issued by the U.S. Bureau of Waits and Measures.

It turns out Americans spend a lot of time waiting. We spend 18 hours a year waiting for elevators, 32.5 hours waiting in lines, 14 hours trapped in voice-mail hell screaming into a phone where there is no one to listen to a single word we say, between 17 and 19 hours waiting for Web sites to come up, and 364 days waiting for sex.

We also spend much of our time eating. The only thing that takes longer than the 7 hours we spend each week eating dinner is the 8 hours we spend weekly purchasing and eating fast food. Including breakfast, snacks, kicking coin machines that take our money and don't give us a thing, staring at candy counters to make a decision, trying to understand why chocolate bars continue to get smaller as the price increases, and trying to convince ourselves that we really like the taste of granola, overall, we spend almost 700 hours annually eating. Of that, 6 six are spent eating healthy foods. We also spend 340 hours exercising to lose the weight that we gained in that 700 hours, 32 hours consulting diet books, 12 hours selecting low-fat meals, and 68 hours watching weight-loss infomercials.

If Americans ceased eating, we would get back almost 50 full days of free time!

As it turns out, Americans spend almost 1,000 hours annually on sex. That includes 600 hours thinking about it, 150 hours reading about it, 150 hours wishing we could get some, 26 hours making up phony descriptions to be used in answering personal ads like "Sophia Loren look-alike" or "ruggedly handsome" when in reality it should read "still breathing," 13 hours lying to friends about getting it, 10 hours of phone sex, 41 hours in close personal relationships with ourselves, and 15 hours of real sex.

We spend more time in the bathroom than in any other room with the exception of the bedroom. In addition to brushing their teeth, men spend 30.5 hours combing their hair. Bald or partially bald men spend only 10 hours combing their hair, while partially bald men with a combover spend 40.7 hours getting it just right so nobody except every person in the entire world will know that they are trying to cover up that they have no hair.

We actually spend 30 minutes a day in the john,

except for men with three or more children, who spend 2.1 minutes. Teenaged boys—everybody knows what they're doing in there—and my uncle Pete—no one can figure out what he's doing—spend at least one hour a day locked in there.

We watch a lot of television. We spend 950 hours watching television, of which 5 hours are spent watching *Twilight Zone* reruns, 11 hours are spent complaining that *Saturday Night Live* is never as funny as it was with the original cast and they still don't know how to end a skit, .5 hours watching national news, and about 5 minutes watching political debates because we know they're all liars anyway and no one with half a mind would believe them so we're better off spending 21 hours watching *The Simpsons* and 4.8 hours reading stories that Calista Flockhart is anorexic.

We spend 47 hours shopping for material goods and 56 hours bringing material goods in for repair or replacement. We spend 12 hours trying to understand our phone bill, 15 hours trying to figure out how all those crazy things that the phone supposedly does actually work, and 20 hours talking to solicitors who call during dinner to try to convince us to switch our phone service when we can't even remember which company we're using in the first place.

We spend 14.3 hours unsuccessfully programming our VCRs, 8 hours trying to figure out how to turn on the TV after we've accidentally pushed one of the 87 buttons on the remote and it says on the set we've AV/TVR/SAT3 and we're supposed to know what that means.

Men and women with no children spend 1,020 hours on recreation. Men and women with one child spend 500 hours on recreation, with two children 150, and with three children they're minus 100 hours. Couples with more than three children did not have time to respond to this survey.

Computers have cut drastically into our time. We now spend 14.7 hours weekly on our home computers, an increase of 3.8 hours in only two years. Of that time 2.7 hours is spent on business and household items, 4 hours is spent answering E-mail from people you wouldn't speak to on the phone or reading the same jokes five different people sent you, 5.8 is spent playing games while pretending to be working, and the remainder is divided equally between trying to figure out exactly what we did wrong to cause the computer to get screwed up and correct it without having to reboot the entire system, which takes forever and has something to do with something called lost clusters, and trying to get out of mortgage advertisements that attack from out of nowhere and keep coming back like a dog biting your leg that won't let go.

We spend 156 hours annually on home and lawn care, 12 hours totally lost somewhere in Home Depot, 1 hour looking for a stick thin enough to get the dog doo out of the grid on the bottom of our sneakers, and finally, we spent .3 hours annually just relaxing completely and enjoying our home and lawn.

—*Dr. Thomas Fenton Jr.*

The Real Equality

ALL RECENT POLLS HAVE RATED EQUALITY OF THE SEXES AS ONE of the most important social advances of the twentieth century. At the beginning of the century women were not even permitted to vote; by the end of the century they were running for president. In this march to equality there have been many milestones. While some of them—such as the first woman Supreme Court justice or the first woman to be admitted to the private college The Citadel—have received tremendous publicity, some important events equally deserving of attention are not as well known.

- The first woman driver to refuse her husband's request to stop for directions—Mrs. Mary Ann Rogers, last seen outside Las Vegas, Nevada, July 24, 1981.
- The first woman to stare directly at a man's groin during a conversation—Martha Simon, New York City, May 11, 1985.

- The first woman multimillionaire to claim about her much younger boyfriend "I'm just so lucky to find a man really attracted to much older, overweight women"—Marsha Paige, November 28, 1991.
- The first woman race-car driver to run in the Indianapolis 500 and stay in the left lane while never going above forty-five miles per hour—"Steady" Betty O'Brien, May 30, 1995.
- The first woman credited with using the phrase "Slam, bam, thank you, man!"—3,476 women tied for first.
- The first woman to play one down in professional football—the late Joan "the Bouncer" Johnson, October 23, 1987.
- The first woman to come home from work with after-shave lotion on her blouse and tell her husband it was just from one of the boys in the mail room—Mrs. Helen Williamson, vice president, the L.T.J. Corporation, Long Island City, New York, May 9, 1990.
- The first woman to tell a man seriously "It's not you, it's me"—Donna Davis, Minneapolis, Minnesota, March 23, 1985.
- The first woman to tell her husband "I don't have a headache. I just want to go to sleep"—Emma Peabody, Bangor, Maine, August 28, 1985.
- The first woman admitted to The Citadel to flunk a course—Lynn Alice Edwards, who flunked men's basketball, November 10, 1997.
- The first *Playboy* centerfold to claim she posed naked only because she needed the money to continue her college education—Gloria Harper, Miss August, 1954.

- The first woman to claim she bought *Playgirl* for the articles—June Maye Johnson, Amarillo, Texas, January 12, 1992.
- The first woman to tell her husband "Don't you dare call a plumber. I can fix this leak easy"—Mrs. Francis Thomas, Baltimore through Bethesda, Maryland, July 26–August 6, 1988.
- First woman to refuse to stop at a gas station and subsequently run out of gas—Mrs. Kathy Cummings, Great Falls, Montana, September 19, 1994.
- The first woman to belch in public then proudly pat her stomach—Dale Smith, San Francisco, California, May 10, 1983.
- The first woman to be arrested for exposing herself to men—to be announced.

The Seven Secrets of Highly Rich People

STUDIES HAVE SHOWN THAT RICH PEOPLE HAVE SOMETHING most of us do not: money.

For many Americans, life revolves around their economic stability. We do many things for income that we would not do if given the choice. We work at jobs that are not satisfying. We speak with wealthy relatives who are really boring. And we buy lottery tickets and imagine that we might win knowing realistically we have more chance of being elected king of England than winning the jackpot.

But many people have earned considerable fortunes through the use of smart business strategies. And there is a belief that by better understanding how they did so we might successfully follow their path. So in the quest to learn how rich people earned their money, authors Jordan Langsam and Daniel Fisher spoke to scores of extremely wealthy people. They found the answer could be condensed into seven secrets:

1. Don't tell anybody anything about anything.
2. Especially don't tell the IRS anything.
3. Never respond to writers' questions for interviews about how you earned your money.
4. If the writers call, have your secretary tell them that you're out of the country and she doesn't know when you'll be back.
5. Don't let your relatives know anything about your financial situation; especially your husband or wife.
6. If Donald Trump wants to claim credit, let him.
7. Remember, there is no such thing as a secret if more than one person knows it.

Old Yeller

SOMETIMES, IN THE MYSTERY OF THE EARLY-MORNING LIGHT, my eyes fool me and I think I see him lying there in his favorite spot on the carpet. But as my eyes adjust to reality, I realize it's just a trick of my memory, and it's just the spot he wore down. Oh, I remember those mornings so well; I'd be rushing down the stairs to get ready to go to school and Gramps would be lying there, right where he'd passed out after coming home late the night before. I'd step carefully over him and go into the kitchen, warmed by the gentle bluster of his snores.

Old Yeller, we all lovingly called him, 'cause it seemed that he was always screaming at us about something, but he was our gramps, and as I grew up, he was always there for us—and it wasn't just because he had nowhere else to go.

He had a lot to do with making me the person I am today, and often, when the bartender announces last call, I'll hoist a good cold one for him and say, "This one's for you, Gramps." It was Gramps, for example, who taught me the importance of being self-reliant. Many times when I would go to him with one of my homework problems, he'd scream at me, "Go do it yourself," his way of reminding me that to survive in this rough world we must all learn how to do things for ourselves.

When I was young, Gramps was always testing me, making sure my mind was working. He was always asking me questions like "What's my name again?" or "Where am I?" And as I got a bit older, his questions became bigger, forcing me to think about the world. One morning as I stepped over him lying on the floor, he opened one eye and asked, "What am I doing here?"

Greater men than I have wrestled with that question for lifetimes. The best I could say was "This is right where you fell down when you came home from the tavern, Gramps."

A lot of things about Grandpa weren't immediately obvious. He was a lot smarter than he liked to let on. For example, I often heard him speaking a foreign language that no one else even understood. And he was tough; he could roll down an entire staircase then just get up and stumble away.

All my friends loved Gramps. He liked to play that he was just a gruff old man, but I knew how much he enjoyed making us kids laugh. Sometimes just watching him try to stand up would send us all into a laughing fit. Then he would pretend to get all riled up and start to chase us. Well, he would act crazy, as if he couldn't go more than a few feet toward one of us without falling down, or after taking several steps, he'd suddenly turn and go in another direction. We'd be laughing so hard we couldn't have moved even if he had been able to get to us, but somehow he never did. And then, just to make things even funnier, at times he'd "accidentally" loosen his belt buckle so that when he started to run after us, his pants would fall down round his knees and then he'd go flopping straight down right after them.

And it was Gramps who taught me how to deal with those times when things get really bad, when I'm feeling so sad and depressed and I don't know if I can deal with my problems. Fact is, things were often hard around our house. Sometimes money got real short, what with my mother and father having to support five kids as well as Gramps. But no matter how tough things got, even when there were barely scraps on the table and we were all hungry, Gramps would just open a bottle of his special "medicine," and before long he was as happy as if he were a millionaire. He'd be singing out of tune and laughing loudly, and I'd look at him admiringly and think, with all he's got going against him, he's still a happy man.

Gramps died a long time ago, but I still miss him. And there are times, in the dark afternoons when the wind blows just right through the trees, that if I listen carefully enough, I can once again hear him saying the three most beautiful words in the English language to me: "Hit me again!"

—*Tony Travis*

A Scents Memory

As I was walking down our street last week, I was suddenly struck by the unmistakable aroma of my childhood. Someone nearby was burning a pile of leaves. That easily recognizable smell raised warm and wonderful feelings, and I was instantly transported back to my own backyard. After my brothers and sisters and I had raked all the leaves in the backyard into one big pile, we'd all drink warm cider as Dad burned them in a great bonfire. Then we'd hold hands in a big circle and dance around the fire.

The ability of scents to ignite memories is powerful. A whiff of sweet perfume is a memory of my mother getting ready to go out with Dad for dinner. The smell of a cigar is the security of my father relaxing in the den after a long day of work and a pleasant dinner.

It seems these days that almost every breeze carries with it a memory. At a party recently I met an old friend who had been drinking. One whiff of his breath and I was once again back home with my brothers and sisters, and I could detect that same strong smell on Dad's breath as we snuggled safely in our hidey-holes while he searched the house, screaming for us to come out.

It rained not long ago and our big German shepherd came into the house all wet, and just one little sniff of his wet fur brought me all the way back to the day our old cat, Marty, got caught in the rain and Mom tried to dry him out in the microwave. Boy, the smell of that explosion is something I'll never forget.

I love to garden, and this past spring when I got down on my hands and knees to plant fresh vegetables, I was overwhelmed by the heavenly scent of newly turned earth. Within seconds I was my small self again, wondering where Mom had disappeared to for the past three weeks.

Sometimes it seems as if every smell leads to home— dirty dishes piling up in the sink, soiled laundry lying on the floor, the unmistakable aroma of food that has been left out too long rotting in the sunlight. Sometimes one smell leads invariably to another. For me, at least, the scent of a lit cigarette leads invariably to the dank odor of my ten-year-old brother throwing up after finishing his first pack.

The ability of one short puff of air to trigger a host of memories is remarkable. I recently singed a few hairs on my arm while lighting a candle, and I could just as easily have been back in the kitchen as Mom shoved my brother into the stove accidentally setting his hair on fire. Using the men's room at a gas station, the moment I opened the door it was as if I were standing in our basement and there was Uncle Mark passed out on the floor.

Different perfumes bring forth a host of memories. My wife recently put on a new sweet scent she'd bought, and it could just as easily have been my father coming home late at night after working hard at the office. Or when I walk past my secretary, just the slightest breeze carrying her floral aroma instantly brings me back to her apartment for the first time only four or five short years ago.

A thousand smells every day bring back all the days of my life. Each time I fill my car with gasoline, I could just as easily be in my old store the night of the big fire. When someone opens a bathroom door, I am right back in the cell in which I spent two long years.

But some scents are far more meaningful to me than others. When I'm overwhelmed by the aroma of freshly oiled machinery, for example, in my mind I can just see those brand-new $20 bills coming off the printing press and remember the moment when I first experienced the sweet smell of success.

—Mark Mackay

The Hidden Dangers of Technology

WE ARE IN THE MIDST OF THE GREATEST TECHNOLOGICAL REV-
olution in the history of mankind. As A hundred years
ago affordable electricity changed the world, bringing
us such wonders as the electric light and the electric
chair and Dennis Rodman's hair, so the microchip is
shaping a new society. The proliferation of technology
has made possible instant communication, made available in our homes more information than is contained
in all the libraries of the world, and offered us incredible new forms of entertainment. But for all these
advantages, there has been a price.

Lost in the excitement has been the new dangers created by this technology. While the media has focused on
the advances, the dark secret of progress has been the
damage done to countless lives. Medical problems such
as carpal tunnel syndrome are well-known, but others
are far more dangerous. Cell phones, for example,
enable us to speak to anyone at any time from any-

where. But as Frank Hamblen of New York City discovered, cell phones can be extremely hazardous.

The cell phone industry doesn't tell consumers stories like this. But in November 1999 Hamblen and his wife were in a Broadway theater, having paid top price of $150 a ticket and having waited several months to see the controversial Pulitzer Prize–winning drama *The Secret of Life*. Incredibly, at the climactic moment in the play, just as star Kevin Spacey was about to reveal the incredible secret of life—Hicker's cell phone started ringing loudly!

It took five emergency-room doctors laboring through the night to prove that a man could actually swallow a cell phone and survive!

Computers have changed innumerable lives for the better—but not all. In the wrong hands, a computer can be a dangerous weapon. Martin Bellow, a $175,000-a-year vice president of marketing at Great Graphics! in Pasadena, California, was a virtuoso at the computer, a master of programming. There was nothing he couldn't do at his computer. But his personal life was not as well controlled. Unbeknownst to his wife, he had been seeing another woman for almost a year—and unbeknownst to that woman, he had recently begun seeing someone else. One afternoon, he confessed these transgressions to a close friend in an E-mail, pouring out his heart key by key. But just as he finished, he reached across his computer for his cup of coffee. Unfortunately, his hand slipped and accidently hit two keys.

Until that moment no one knew for sure the scope of the entire Microsoft network. Bellow's E-mail made him famous. He even made legal history when the judges in both his divorce and palimony cases ruled that this E-mail could be used as evidence.

In the early days of this revolution most devices could easily be controlled by a simple on-and-off switch. But as the capabilities of simple devices increased, it became increasingly difficult to control them. Thomas Dunne of Newport News, Virginia, considered himself an extremely competent man. Having finished graduate courses in both computer science and VCR programming, he took great pride in his ability to get the most out of the electronic devices in his home and office. But while visiting friends in San Diego who had a complete media room, Dunne made the mistake of staying up to watch television after his host went to bed. According to police estimates, it was soon after the late-night news, at approximately 11:30 P.M., that Dunne made his initial attempt to turn off the television set.

Unfortunately, this television set was connected to a satellite dish, computer monitor, VCR, and DVD player. Dunne unsuccessfully worked through the night attempting to uncover the proper sequence to turn it off. They found him sitting in front of the set the next morning, pressing buttons and mumbling incoherently, "I can do this, I'm a grown human being, I know I can turn off a television set . . ."

When admitted to the Thomas A. Edison Clinic for the Technically Incompetent for intensive therapy, Dunne was still clutching the remote control, claiming, "I can do this. I know I can do this . . ."

It was to be a night to remember for Chris Kelly. He had arranged for a limousine to pick him up and drive to his girlfriend's house. They were to go to an exclusive restaurant, and at the end of the dinner he would propose marriage to her. At seven o'clock he was dressed and ready to go; the only thing he needed was additional cash to pay for various services. The limousine driver stopped at an ATM machine and Kelly entered his access code.

Or so he thought. "Invalid entry. Please try again," the ATM informed him. Kelly tried it again—and got the same response. Kelly was certain this was the proper number; it consisted of his birthday and his address. He thought, maybe I've got them in the wrong order, and he reversed the digits. "Please try again," the machine said. He could feel himself getting angry, but tried again. And again. He was getting confused, maybe it wasn't his birthday, he decided, maybe it was his confirmation date. He entered the new code numbers.

"Please try again," the machine mocked him.

Behind him a line of people anxious to get their money were stirring. Kelly tried again. And again he was told—wrong number. He looked at his watch. It was almost time to be at the restaurant, and he hadn't even picked up his girlfriend. As he punched in the next set of numbers, he felt beads of sweat running down his spine. He tried again and again and again.

"Please try again," the machine insisted politely. Finally, he couldn't take it anymore. He punched the machine. "Gimme my money," he screamed. Then he kicked it. "It's my money. I want it!" he yelled as he kicked it again and again. "Mine, I tell you, it's mine . . ."

He was still kicking the machine when the police arrived. Chris Kelly was arrested for destruction of private property. His girlfriend, believing she had been stood up, broke up with him. They never spoke again.

Like so many people before him, like Bellow and Dunne and untold thousands of others, that night Chris Kelly became just another victim of modern technology.

The Future Is in Front of Us

The most difficult thing about being an American Jew is that there are two New Year's Eves on which I can't get a date!

—JOSH RUBIN

INCREDIBLY, MORE THAN FOUR HUNDRED YEARS AGO THE LEGendary French seer Nostradamus correctly predicted that the twentieth century would end on December 31, 1999! While Nostradamus's predictions are somewhat vague and thus open to interpretation, according to some experts he also successfully predicted that a women's revolution would begin at the Broadhurst Theatre in February 1975 over complaints about the long lines outside the ladies' room during intermission, the total collapse of the Philadelphia Phillies at the end of the 1964 baseball season, and the final grosses of *Scream 2!*

Making these predictions even more amazing was that Nostradamus had at his disposal only the tools of his time: a pencil, parchment, and a funny-looking hat with a lot of stars and a half-moon on it.

The science of guessing the future has progressed tremendously from those years. Prognosticators have used everything from tarot cards to bones to the lines

on an individual's palm to tell the future. Modern seers
have adapted the tools of our society to the foretelling
of the future. Sasha Stallone, for example, the mother
of actor Sylvester Stallone, has people sit naked on
copy machines and then reads the printout. But many
other people have discovered they have the unique
ability to tell the future by examining the evidence of
the present.

One of the most unusual seers is auto mechanic Jim
Bagley of Dallas, Texas. Two years ago a woman named
Joanne Wanamaker drove her car, which was leaking
oil, into Bagley's shop for repairs. The car sat there for
several hours as Bagley prepared for work. Bagley
watched in amazement as a large oil slick formed on
the floor in an unusual shape. Then, after carefully
examining this oil slick, Bagley corrected predicted,
"This is going to cost you a whole shitload of money!"

Two days later the final bill came to $658! Bagley
claims that this was his first look into the future, but
since that time he has successfully read oil slicks with
uncanny accuracy.

Boston, Massachusetts, housewife Pam Bell has
become well known for successfully foretelling the
future of relationships. Women have been consulting
her to find out whether they will have a satisfying relationship with the man they are dating. Bell asks that
they bring with them three things from the man: a snip
of his hair, a small sample of the cologne he uses, and
his bankbook. From only those items she is able to predict with uncanny accuracy the potential for success in
a new relationship.

Rather than reading tea leaves, Mendocino, California,
resident Marte Stallings has been reading marijuana

leaves for six years. Her record thus far is not particularly good, but the truth is no one seems to care.

Some people have used these modern tools to predict their own future with uncanny success. Atlanta, Georgia, cardiologist Dr. Kent Nelson was able to read electrocardiograms and successfully predict the size of his house and new swimming pool. In Minneapolis, Minnesota, after being married to her husband for twenty-six years, Mrs. Diane Forbush was able to determine from the shape of a lipstick stain on her husband's collar that she would soon be obtaining a large amount of jewelry. And incredibly, David Potter of Chicago, Illinois, was able to predict from the number of times his son played the same rap song at top volume on his CD player that within days he would have a nervous breakdown. In fact, his son swears that his father actually told him beforehand, "If I have to listen to that song one more time, I'm going to go crazy!"

To put the amazing ability of amateur fortune-tellers to correctly predict the future in context, the U.S. Weather Bureau has approximately $170 million worth of sophisticated measuring devices in place, supported by banks of superfast computers to decipher that information—and the best predictions they are able to make is "A chance of showers!"

—*Charles Kaufman*

My Little Brother

THESE DAYS IT'S PRETTY HARD NOT TO THINK ABOUT MY LITTLE brother every time I get into a car. While he was always younger than me, I've never met anyone quite like him. He made such a strong impact on people's lives. I don't think anyone who met him ever forgot him. Maybe a lot of other people considered him crazy, but to me he was just mildly odd.

I guess what I remember best growing up were the countless hours we shared in the backseat of the car. It seemed as if Dad and Mom were always getting us up in the middle of the night, packing our belongings in the car, and taking us for long drives.

Sometimes it got boring just sitting back there, and so my brother was always thinking up games for us to play to while away the long hours. We played all the traditional car games: license plate—competing to see who could spot cars from the most different states—we played name that car, we played the alphabetical animal game, we played spell it backwards, twenty questions, and even the "What's this coming out of my nose?" game. But when we got tired of playing those games, my brother would invent new games that the whole family could play.

I'll certainly never forget the first game he invented, Surprise the Driver! Dad was driving on the highway when my little brother suddenly leaped forward and clamped both his hands over Dad's eyes and screamed right in his ear, "Surprise!" Boy, Dad certainly was surprised! The object of the game, as my little brother explained, was to wait until the driver had forgotten we were playing—then surprise him. We would invent all sorts of fun ways of doing that. One night, I remember, the car was very quiet when I suddenly screamed the warning, "Watch out for that guy, Dad!" and pointed straight ahead to where absolutely no one was walking.

Dad managed to quickly regain control of the car. When we all stopped laughing, my little brother admitted, "That's worth seven points."

But I guess my brother's best surprise was lighter fluid in the ashtray. He just put a little bit of lighter fluid in the ashtray and waited until Mom went to put out her cigarette. That was definitely a ten-pointer!

Another game my brother invented was Name That Sound. The object was to put something somewhere in the car that would make a noise. The first person to identify it won. Marbles in the glove compartment was easy, firecrackers in the exhaust pipe was more difficult, but the hardest one of all was the cat in the engine. It took us an hour to guess that one.

A game I always loved to play with my brother was Mirror Mirror. We bought a mirror with our allowance, and at night we would use it to reflect the headlights of the car right behind us back into that driver's eyes. Sometimes we could even see the stunned look on the driver's eyes before he lost control.

My brother just made the hours we spent in that car go by so fast. As we got older, the games got a little more complicated. A game he loved much more than I did was Which Wire Did I Cut? When we stopped for gas or to eat, one of us would cut one wire without telling Mom or Dad. We were only allowed to cut one wire, which we had to pick at random. And then we would each guess what that wire did. The fun part of that game was not knowing exactly when the function of the wire would be revealed, whether it would be the first time Dad put on the brakes or while we were driving across the desert.

I don't think Dad liked our games at first, but after a while he got into it and started inventing his own games. He invented games like Kidnapped, in which he bound and gagged us and put us in the trunk and we had to get free, and Where Am I, in which he left us blindfolded on a corner and we had to figure out where we were.

Sometimes I miss those old days. Today, whenever I turn on the engine of my own car, I always think about my little brother. I haven't heard from him in a long time, since his escape from the institution. But every day I scan the papers looking for some hint where he might be—and every time I read about a strange accident I wonder if I've found him.

—*Meredith Ann McIntosh*

A Cat's-Eye View of Dogs

In the award-winning novella *Conversations with My Cat*, a cat named Bomber is asked why cats have such deep enmity toward dogs:

His eye whiskers stood straight up. "What's so awful about being a dog?" he repeated incredulously. "Are you kidding me? Have you ever seen a dog?" He almost spit out the word *dog*, although his lack of lips prevented him from actually spitting. "Dogs are an embarrassment to their entire species," he began. "The way they'll roll over for a few measly crumbs off the table. Or play dead when a human tells them to. Dead? What kind of game is dead? They lie down and don't move, and people think it's a trick. Believe me, I know dogs, it's not a trick. It's what they do best— nothing!

"And that's supposed to show how smart dogs are? Makes me wonder how smart humans are. You ever see a cat play dead? Absolutely not. And why not?

Because cats have integrity and self-respect. We have pride in our genus. Where do you think the word *pride* came from? You ever hear anyone talk about a 'pride of dogs'? I don't believe so."

He was terribly agitated. Obviously he'd been holding this anger inside for a long time. I couldn't calm him down.

He hopped down from his chair and paced rapidly around the room as he continued, "Dogs actually believe people respect them. I've heard them say that so many times. Do you believe that? How dumb can they be? They've sold their souls to humans, and for what? I'll tell you. When one human wants to threaten another human with the worst possible thing he can do, what does he say? He's going to turn him into 'dog meat.' That's what people really think about dogs. And what do humans call the worst time of the year, when it's too hot to even move and all you can do is lie there? 'The dog days.' Does that show any respect for dogs? No, it does not. But do dogs care? They don't even realize it. They're a disgrace. I mean, you've heard humans saying, 'Lie down with dogs and you get up with fleas.' Is that supposed to be a compliment? Maybe I'm missing something here, but that's what people really think about dogs. They think they're animals.

"But does this bother dogs? Not at all. They're oblivious. You notice you've heard of a 'dog catcher' but you've never heard of a 'cat catcher.' Know why? Because dogs have a psychological need to be caught. To be put on a leash and treated like a prisoner. It makes them feel wanted.

"And then if they do get loose, what do they do?

They chase cars. Cars! How incredibly stupid can they be? What would they possibly do with a car if they caught one? Have you ever seen a dog eating a car? No, you have not. Have you ever even seen a dog bring a car home? No, you haven't. After all these years, you'd think by now at least one dog somewhere might have figured out that there is absolutely no reason to chase cars. But, no, they insist on doing it, as if they think they're going to catch one and all of a sudden it's going to turn into a huge hamburger." He added in a high-pitched voice, presumably his imitation of a dumb dog, "Oh, no! Metal again."

He continued walking in a large circle around the couch. "Dogs don't understand that people don't respect them. But, I mean, it's so obvious. When a human does something wrong, where do they send him? To the doghouse. But when a man wants pleasure, where does he go? To the cathouse. When a man does something wrong, they say he's a dog. But when he does something good, he's a cool cat. See? See what I'm trying to explain to you?

"And this scam about dogs being man's best friend? Oh, please. You know why they're man's best friend? Because they never ask to borrow anything, they never make any demands, they never want to discuss their personal problems, and they never complain. They're happy to eat dog food and live in the doghouse. Sure, I'd want a dog as my best friend, too.

"But, no, dogs aren't interested in being *my* best friend. In fact, when they're not busy chasing cars, they like to chase cats up trees. And you know why? Because they're bullies, that's why. They have to show their human masters how tough they are by picking on someone smaller than they are, so they take out all their frustrations on us. But even that doesn't work. They never catch us, because they're always barking up the wrong tree."

What terrible thing could have happened to him in his kittenhood, I wondered, to have engendered this hostility? When he finally settled down, I asked, "Well, Bomber, isn't there anything good you can say about dogs?"

He considered the question for several moments. And finally he decided, "Well, I guess there's one thing. At least they're not chickens. And don't get me started on chickens!"

—*an excerpt from* Conversations with My Cat

An Act of Courage

IT WAS THE MOST DIFFICULT DAY OF MY LIFE. I HAD BEEN WAITing anxiously for the cast of our high school musical, *South Pacific*, to be announced, fully expecting that I would win the lead role of nurse Nellie Forbush. I'd already been working with a private music teacher on several of the songs. But when the list was posted, a girl who had recently moved into our small town was given the part. I was relegated to the chorus.

As soon as I saw the list, I started crying. I was embarrassed and humiliated. I'd told so many people I expected to win the role that I didn't think I could ever show my face in that school again. It was so totally gross. The new girl wasn't even popular or pretty. She didn't even have her own car!

I was still crying when I got home. Between sobs I managed to tell my mother what had happened. "Momma, it isn't fair. This meant everything to me. I'll never get over it."

She hugged me tightly. "It's okay, sweetheart. It's not

the end of the world. You know, there's a good lesson here for you to learn."

"Oh, you just don't understand."

"You'd be surprised. Did I ever tell you what happened to me my senior year?"

I stopped crying. "No, you didn't." My mother rarely talked about her childhood.

"Well, just like you I was a very good actress," she said sincerely. "Our senior class play was *Our Town*, and I knew I had earned the right to play the lead. But when the cast was announced, a girl I didn't know very well, a girl who came from across the railroad tracks, had won the part."

"Oh, Mom, why didn't you ever tell me this?"

"Hush," she said, holding up her index finger to her lips. "Well, I immediately confronted the drama teacher and asked her why. And she told me, 'I know you expected to get the part, and maybe you should have. But Mary's mother just died, her father is very sick, and she's been diagnosed with a progressive eye disease. She's going blind. This might be the last chance she'll ever have to do something like this, and I hoped you would understand.'"

"Oh, Mama, how terrible."

"Yes, it was, but I still didn't give up hope I could get the part."

I was so surprised. I had never known my mother was that determined. "Well, what happened?"

"First, I befriended that girl. I got to know her real well. *Real* well, if you know what I mean. And just before every rehearsal I'd be sure to ask her about her sick father. Then I'd hold up three fingers and ask her how many fingers I was holding up."

"Could she still see them?"

"Oh, yeah, so I had to lie about the right answer. Day by day I could see her confidence dwindling. We started rehearsing together at my house, and every few days I'd replace the lightbulb with one a little less bright. Gradually she became convinced that her sight was going even faster than the doctors had warned.

"Everybody at school thought I was wonderful for helping her play the part I wanted so badly. They thought I was even nicer when I got angry about those nasty rumors being spread about how Mary got the part."

"What rumors?"

"That was the beauty of it. There weren't any. So when I stood up and said angrily, 'If I find out who's spreading the rumor that Mary . . . ,' well, you know, sweetheart."

"So did Mary finally drop out of the play?"

"I wouldn't exactly call it dropping out. It was more like tripping down a flight of stairs."

"Mama!"

She looked at me sheepishly. "Well, what else could I do? I stepped in at the last minute and saved the play."

When I got to school the next day, I immediately went to find my new best friend. "How are you feeling?" I asked her happily—as I put my arm protectively around her shoulders.

—*Belle Stevens*

Uncle Jake's Will

I DON'T THINK ANY OF US REALIZED WHAT A WISE MAN UNCLE Jake was until the day the lawyer read his will. When he was alive, Uncle Jake adamantly refused to discuss his will with anyone. He would often insist, "I'm not going to talk about my will." But once each year, the day after his birthday, he would put on his best suit and march right down to that lawyer's office. "A man's got to keep current" was what he said, but we understood he was "making adjustments."

We never even knew how rich Uncle Jake was. The rumors about his riches were so old we didn't even know where they'd started. But we had grown up hearing about some mysterious investments that had worked out, or an unexpected inheritance from a friend to whom he had been unexpectedly kind. All we did know was that every holiday and on our birthdays he would give us each a shiny silver dollar.

In truth, Uncle Jake wasn't a happy man. He seemed to be angry at the world. He never married so we were the only real family he had, but even with us he could be pretty nasty and cutting. Although we never brought up the subject, I remember he used to tell us, "I know that the only reason you come to visit me is because of my will. That's not necessary. I don't want anyone spending time with me just because they think they might get a lot of money."

We would insist that wasn't the case. In fact, every time I saw him I would insist that wasn't the case. "I really don't care about your money, Uncle Jake. I come to see you more than anyone else in the family because I really want to."

I'm sure my brothers and sisters didn't care about that money just as much as I didn't. Although admittedly there were times when we would speculate on the size of his fortune and talk about who was currently in favor or who was about to be written out of the will. And like me, from time to time I'm sure the rest dreamed of how their life would be changed if they were the "favorite" niece or nephew.

Uncle Jake lived a long time. A long, long time. And each of us dutifully went to see him as he failed, taking special care each time to reassure him that we were there because we loved him and not because he might be kind to us in his will.

Two months after his passing we gathered in the lawyer's office for the reading of that will. We all sat there nervously as the lawyer opened the safe-deposit box. Then he cleared his throat and read Uncle Jake's final will and testament. And that's when I realized how wise he really was. "Hey, I never said I had a fortune," he had written, "because I don't. But I'd like to thank each of you for coming to see me so often." And he left each of us one silver dollar.

I learned a great lesson from Uncle Jake. In truth, I had been going to see him because I, too, hoped to be remembered in this will. But as I look back on that day, I realize I had learned an important lesson from him: it isn't what's in a person's will that makes the difference, it's what people think is in that will.

And so I can say to Uncle Jake, thanks for nothing.

—Larry Carty

The Gimme Tree

ONCE A LITTLE BOY WAS WALKING THROUGH THE FOREST behind his house. As he walked down a path, a tree grabbed his shirt with its long, tangly branches and would not let go. "Hey," said the boy, "what do you want from me?"

"I'm really thirsty," the tree said. "Gimme some water and in return I'll give you some shade in the summer."

So the boy fetched water for the tree and the tree was happy.

In the summer when the boy came for his shade, the tree tripped him with one of its long roots. "Hey," said the boy, brushing himself off, "what do you want from me?"

"It's getting too crowded around here," said the tree. "I want you to gimme a little space. Cut down all the other trees around me and in return I'll make my leaves the most brilliant colors you've ever seen in the fall."

"Jeez," the boy said, "why do I always have to find talking trees." But he cut down all the other trees and the tree was happy.

In the fall when the boy came back to see the brilliant colors, the tree dropped acorns and apples on his head. "Hey, com'on," the boy said, rubbing his head, "now what do you want from me?"

"These birds on my branches are driving me crazy. Chirp, chirp, chirp, all day and all night. Gimme a break. I'm telling you, I'm going nuts here. I want you to get rid of them for me."

"What are you offering this time?"

"How 'bout I don't break off some branches in a windstorm that maybe fall on your house, if you know what I mean?"

"Are you threatening me?"

"Hey, I'm a tree. I've got limited resources here. What do you expect me to do?"

So the little boy sighed and climbed the tree and shooed off all the birds. Then he rubbed his cat in a towel and rubbed the branches with same towel. Because birds have birdbrains, they were scared by the cat smell. And once again the tree was happy.

After the next big storm when the boy's house was safe, he went to visit the tree. Leaves blew in the boy's face. "Now just cut that out," the boy said. "What's your problem now?"

"Take a whiff. All the dogs and cats think I'm a fire hydrant. You got to gimme protection from them."

"I don't know, what do you got to offer me?"

The tree was silent for a long time, then he finally said, "How 'bout your reputation? Maybe I look old to you, kid, but the fact is I'm still growing up. I'm going to be right here for a long time, long after you're gone. Now, if I was to say one or two things about you . . . I mean, you really want people to know you wear girls' clothes?"

The little boy was angry. "But I don't wear girls' clothes!"

"That's your story. But a hundred years from now, who's gonna be there to argue with me? Nah, you'll be known forever as the little boy in the pretty dress."

"You're the meanest tree I've ever met." But the little boy gathered thorns from bushes and laid them all around the tree, and when the dogs and cats came, they stepped on them and never came back. Once again the tree was happy.

A year later the little boy was walking in the forest when his feet got caught in goo and he could barely move. The goo was gum and syrup from the tree. "Hey," he shouted, "what is wrong with you, huh? Why don't you just leave me alone?"

"All right, I admit it. I'm lonely, okay?"

"Well, of course you're lonely. First you had me cut down all the other trees, then you made me get rid of the birds that landed on your branches, then you made me get rid of all the dogs and cats. Duh! There's nobody left. So now what do you want from me, Mr. Know-It-All Tree?"

The tree spoke in a soft breeze. "Your word. Gimme your word that every once in a while you'll come back to visit me."

"Or else what this time?"

"No, I got nothing up my trunk, and maybe you could bring some friends too. Even a dog once in a while wouldn't be so bad. A small one, you know. And I suppose I could live with a bird's nest or two."

"You know, you haven't been very nice to me."

"You're right, and I'm sorry. So whattya say?"

So the little boy gave the tree his word that he would return, and the tree was so happy for a long time that it just grew and grew and grew. For it had learned an important lesson: sometimes it's not so bad to take a little crap from every animal in the forest.

—*Larry Kimball*

The Nineties Anthem

WALL STREET CLERK BEAU STEVENS LEANED AGAINST THE WALL for support and surveyed the incredible mess on the floor of the stock exchange. Minutes earlier the Dow Jones average had shot up over the 10,000 mark for the first time in history. As the bell in the background was sounded to end the trading day, all around him men and women were screaming and pounding each other on the back. Stevens was exhausted, his ears were ringing, his fingers cramped. But in the bright lights of the celebration, he wrote down these few words that will live forever as the anthem for the 1990s:

What's in It for Me?

When a friend is in a jam
And asks you for a helping hand
Before you act irrationally
Ask yourself—what's in it for me?

There's a single thought we so quickly perceive
Giving is fine, but I'd rather receive.
Ask for something ma-ter-ial
Something you can quickly sell.

For it's not the gift, it's the thought that counts
So long as it comes in large amounts.
(Repeat)

When to a friend a favor you bring
Wait to hear that cash register ring.
Before you settle for cheers or applause
Remember you're your very best cause.

'Cause people everywhere are all the same
They prefer straight cash to promised fame.
So take your time and see the U.S.A.
But whatever you do, don't forget to pay.

For it's not the gift, it's the thought that counts
So long as it comes in large amounts.
(Repeat)

Making Books

THIS IS THE STORY OF TWO VERY DIFFERENT BOOKS.

The first book took more than a decade to write. Peter Hayman, a professor at a respected Southern university, believed that books that glorified violence should not be published because they contributed to the growing incidence of violent acts in our society. He spent almost twelve years collecting specific examples in which a violent act could be traced directly to a book. His finished manuscript was almost six hundred pages long and included excerpts from more than forty books, ranging from pulp fiction to nonfiction descriptions of brutality and torture.

Unfortunately, when he read his final draft, he realized that it contained precisely the material his research had concluded should not be published. Faced with the dilemma of having spent twelve years writing a book that argued forcefully against its own existence, he froze at his desk.

He was found there the following morning and was

granted a full scholarship to the Betty Ford Clinic. The book, tentatively titled *Don't Read This Book,* was never published.

The second book took only four months to complete. David Bronstein had previously written several self-help and how-to books. His major success had been a book on hypnosis that supposedly hypnotized readers into going out and buying another copy of the book. That book had sold 23,000 copies—all to the same person.

His new book was a compilation of all the health, diet, and exercise tips he had gathered from trainers and nutritionists. Entitled *Good Health Forever,* it sold slowly at first. Only when he changed the title to *How to Not Die,* and added a triple-your-money-back guarantee if the book—when the health regimes outlined were carefully followed—did not keep the reader alive, did sales explode. Within the first year more than 750,000 copies were in print—and as Bronstein advertised, he had yet had to refund a penny.

Two writers, two books—and two very different outcomes.

—*Frank Weimann*

The Incredible Importance
of Creativity

IT WAS A NIGHT I WILL NEVER FORGET. ONCE JACQUES DE LAUREN had been acclaimed as the greatest designer of men's clothing in history. His suits, his jackets, even his pants, were worn by the richest, most celebrated and successful men in the world. He traveled in the most exclusive circles and was invited to the most glittering events. Television programs profiled him and newspapers quoted him. A single word from him could make a career . . . or ruin one.

But then something awful had happened to him. The precise details were never known, but within only a few years he was reduced to designing for retail chains. The Home Products Network began carrying his clothing. It was rumored that he once even appeared at the opening of a mall!

But de Lauren had fought back valiantly. That night he was to reveal his new collection of men's clothes. For him, this was his final opportunity to restore his tarnished reputation and once again take his place at the summit of men's clothing designers.

Known as "de Lauren: The Collection," it began with his new line of suits. As the models walked down that runaway, the spectators were stunned into silence. From the first moments it was obvious that de Lauren was back. Back! In fabrics ranging from cotton to wool, his suits were an amazing array of colors covering the spectrum from charcoal grays to navy blues and black. Included in this collection were both fashionable single-breasted and whimsical double-breasted jackets. The old de Lauren arrogance was evident in his choice of buttons, as these beautiful suits bore both two buttons and a dashing three buttons. The audience had anxiously been awaiting de Lauren's biggest decision: thin lapels or wide lapels?

Incredibly, de Lauren stood firmly in the middle! His lapels were neither too thin nor too narrow, a perfect compromise of good taste. Some men in the audience were so moved by this that it brought tears to their eyes.

No one has ever done pockets to perfection as has de Lauren, and this collection just reinforced that reputation. The pockets added just the perfect touch.

The last hurdle to be cleared for de Lauren were the pants. Would it be expressive cuffs or the more stylish Continental flair? Would the legs be flared or narrow? Loose-fitting or form-fitting? The tension in the tent was so thick it could have been sliced by a knife. Rumors had been rampant for weeks that de Lauren was going to break tradition and opt for cuffs, but no one knew for certain.

Again, de Lauren confounded the entire industry with his bold compromise: pants with cuffs as well as no cuffs! "There is a new freedom in men's clothing," he decreed, "and so the man of the clothes must himself make that choice!"

As de Lauren proved that memorable night, it was not just hype, promotion, and public relations that had made him a star. His talent was obvious in every gray suit. Jacques de Lauren's incredible comeback was complete. His extraordinary creativity had once again revolutionized the extraordinary world of men's fashion.

It was a night no one would ever forget.

—Paulette Satur

The Hard Road to Greatness

SUCCESS DOES NOT COME EASILY. BUT WITH HARD WORK AND dedication it is a road that can be traveled. Here are some of the unlikely people who have made this journey.

He was born into abject poverty in the slums of New York City, the fourth of nine children. His father was an immigrant barber, his mother took in piecework sewing to survive. He spent the early years of his childhood in a cold-water tenement with no indoor plumbing or furnishings. In the sixth grade the principal beat him up and expelled him from school for fighting with his tutor. That was the extent of his formal education. To survive he worked many jobs: in a munitions company, as a paper cutter, a bartender, and a waiter. While working as a waiter, he got into a fight with a customer—who ended up slashing his face three times. Yet he overcame all that adversity to achieve worldwide recognition. By the age of twenty-six that young man had grown up to become the leader of one of the world's largest crime families! He eventually became the most famous gangster in the world, Al Capone!

This man was the son of a cobbler and an ex-serf. He was expelled from school and even changed his name several times. He was arrested six times and escaped from the prison camp four times. He committed a series of robberies including the bombing of a government truck from which $178,000 was stolen. When he was caught with some of that money, he was exiled to Siberia.

Early in his life he answered to the names Soso, Koba, David, Nijeradze, Chijikov, and the name he finally picked, which translates as "man of steel." From those humble beginnings, with incredible dedication he became *Time* magazine's Man of the Year twice and the most repressive leader in history. He's the man who made Communism what it became, he's Joseph Stalin!

This man's father was a blacksmith and his mother an elementary-school teacher. After leaving school he moved to Switzerland, where he was arrested and deported. He eventually went to find work in Austria— and was also expelled. In Italy he was sent to prison. Yet this man eventually overcame those odds to become dictator of Italy. He built the Italian empire and helped start World War II. Incredibly, this man was Benito Mussolini!

This man's father died of a heart attack two months before he was born. Raised by a single mother who sold goods from the front of the house for the first few years of his life, by the time he was three years old he was living in an orphans home. His mother eventually married three times and fought often with his stepfather. As a boy he had no close friends and was considered "withdrawn and socially maladjusted." He failed home economics in seventh grade and finally dropped out of school for good before completing tenth grade.

Yet this man became the most widely recognized assassin of the twentieth century, Lee Harvey Oswald!

A poor student in high school, this man failed the entrance examination to Vienna's Academy of Fine Arts twice! For a time he lived on the streets, sleeping on park benches and in cheap rooming houses. He often begged food from charity kitchens. As a soldier in World War I he rose all the way to corporal. Little in his background suggested his rise to prominence, but by diligence and perseverance he eventually became the most infamous person of the century, Adolf Hitler!

As each of these men proved, there is no tollbooth on the highway to success!

—*Ernest Porter*

Hand-Me-Down Memories

I WAS BORN SEVENTH OF THE NINE KIDS IN MY FAMILY. THE fourth boy. A lot of love was spread around, which helped make up for the lack of money. Dad worked real hard, but it's hard to support nine kids on a supermarket bagger's salary. So pretty much everything in our family got handed down from one kid to the next, everything from clothes to chewed gum.

Every piece of clothing I wore in my childhood had been passed on down to me. I was just really pleased to have clothes; the family who lived down the road a piece had to wear old cartons. Although when I did get in a fight with their oldest boy—we called him Pall Mall 'cause he looked best in their cartons—he did point out, "At least nobody wore my carton before!"

We couldn't be too picky when it came to clothes; both the boys and the girls wore whatever fit with little regard for gender. "Clothes is clothes," my mother used to say. When I complained about wearing a dress, she replied, "What's the matter with you? Why do you

129

think they call it being dressed? Did you ever hear any-body talk about getting panted?"

Often by the time I got a piece of clothing it had been worn by my three older brothers and three sisters. It was patched and faded, and sometimes they had even left little things in the pockets. I'd find all the usual things kids leave in their pockets: pieces of gum and frogs, old scabs, fingernails, used handkerchiefs, hair, pills, notes with reminders on them like "rob a store at the mall." Once I even found a penny! I guess I did what all kids would do—I ate whatever I could and put back the rest for whoever got it after me.

It wasn't easy wearing used clothing. Often the other kids at school would laugh at me and call me funny names like "clown" and "court jester." I took this abuse as long as I could, but sometimes I just couldn't help it and I started fighting. I guess the one advantage I had over them was that I couldn't ruin my good clothes, and my mother never complained when I got my pants dirty—in fact, she couldn't even tell the difference.

I remember the first time I got a new piece of cloth-ing of my own. It was a shirt, marked down in the store to "take it." Maybe to other people it was an "irregu-lar," but to me it felt so good against my skin I never wanted to take it off. So I wore it day and night for weeks; I went to school in it and played ball in it and went running in the fields with it and slept in it. I loved it so much I wouldn't even let my mother wash it. I wanted it to stay new forever. I'll never forget that new-shirt smell. As the weeks went by, that smell got stronger and stronger.

Many years have passed, but I still have that shirt, still new, still unwashed. I don't wear it too often though. I have been fortunate in my life, I can afford all the new clothes I want. But as difficult as those days were, as embarrassed as I was sometimes, the lessons I learned have proved extremely valuable. Lessons I've never forgotten. First, never, ever, wear stripes with plaids. It is oh so gauche. Second, your hemline should always be just a little tiny bit but not too much above the knee. And third, never make fun of the way somebody else is dressed. Because if I could find that little Pall Mall number today, I guarantee I could sell it for a fortune.

—*Dan Majors*

Fun with the Departed

I'M A MORTICIAN. I LIVE WITH MY FAMILY IN THE REAR OF OUR funeral home. Admittedly it's an unusual place to live, but it's spacious and comfortable. For a time I was concerned that a funeral home might be a difficult place to raise my three kids. But as my family discovered, with just a little bit of creativity even a usually somber place such as a funeral parlor could be turned into a fun-filled home.

My father had been strict. There was little laughter around our house. I don't remember his ever playing a single game with me or my sisters. And the truth is, for a long time I was just like him. But then one day I suddenly remembered how much I'd hated his strict rules, how much I wished my family could be like other families, and I vowed to change. From that moment on our little home turned into a place of mirth.

It all started one day when the kids came in the back to see a newly arrived "client." This was a woman in her mid-sixties. When preparing for a funeral, I usually began by applying makeup. I was always careful to be subtle, "just a little dab of life," I called it. But this time, as the kids watched, I asked, "Don't you think she'd look better with bright red lipstick?"

They were stunned. I'd always been so serious. And when I painted her lips bright red, the kids just couldn't believe it. Then I added some eye shadow and thick rouge. "Who wants to give Mrs. Harrison a mustache?" I asked, holding up my makeup kit.

At first the kids were a little reluctant to play, but once they realized how much fun it could be, they happily joined in. Naturally we cleaned up our clients long before the funeral, so no harm was done. Soon my preparation room was filled with the sound of laughter.

That was just the beginning. We invented the most wonderful games. While other kids played doctor, our children played "organ donor." When one of our younger children asked for a "head start" in a game, oh, boy, did we give it to them. Our kids learned the real meaning of "an eye for an eye." In our house, when someone needed a "helping hand," they got it. Sometimes they even got two!

We took all the holidays seriously around our house. For example, on Valentine's Day I always gave my beautiful wife and wonderful kids lovely hearts. But obviously Halloween was always our favorite. We went out of our way to make it memorable, although some years it cost us an arm and a leg. I'm sure some of the kids in our neighborhood will never forget the surprise they got when we opened the door!

I tried hard not to let the kids get too attached to our clients—well, except for that one thing I did with the superglue, of course. So no one ever knew what went on behind the thick, white doors of 149 Strattford Road. But I never forgot that simply by changing the rules I'd brought our family together.

—*Griffin Miller*

The Amazing Dr. Doolittle

And a little child shall lead them: When I told my grandson that a present I'd bought him was guaranteed to last one hundred years, he asked, "How did they test that?"

—RICHARD WOLFE

FEW EULOGIES ARE REMEMBERED QUITE AS WELL AS THIS tribute given by Dr. Ira Fogel to his friend and colleague Dr. Ernest Doolittle.

I am extremely pleased to be here today at the funeral of my friend Dr. Ernest Doolittle. I can honestly say that no one did more than Ernie Doolittle to advance the cause of psychiatric health in this country. Ernie Doolittle believed that bringing together people with similar conditions in small groups could have profound influence on each person. For example, while almost no one believed it was possible to achieve success in dealing with deep cynicism, he persevered. Many people derided his results, but he paid no attention to them.

For Ernie Doolittle was an optimist. Although he himself had grave doubts about his ability to organize groups of optimists, he still made the attempt.

One of the many things I admired about Ernie was his belief that psychiatric help should be available at no cost to people who need it. Although his acclaimed lectures and his television series, *Don't Pay for This,* earned him a small fortune, he remained the same humble man I had always known.

In fact, rather than spending that money on himself, he tried to do some good. To demonstrate his commitment to the conservation movement, for example, he spent much of his fortune tracking and collecting examples of endangered species. Eventually he sponsored a nationwide tour of these rare animals entitled *Wild Things: Let Them Be Free!* for which he gained further acclaim.

His final success in life was the founding of the American Association of Non-Conformists, which brought together for the first time nonconformists and iconoclasts from fifteen nations. Participants in this conference created a system for categorizing unique thinkers into groups, a system that became the foundation of his effort to encourage structured creativity in young people.

There has never been anyone quite like Dr. Ernest Doolittle, and it is my fervent hope that hundreds of people will follow in his footsteps.

—*Richard Soll*

The Littlest Devil

OF ALL THE DEVILS IN CREATION HE WAS THE SMALLEST ONE AND had always been so. At school, all the other young devils would make fun of him and he would get angry; but because they were bigger than him they had bigger powers, so when he tried to call down fire on them, the flames were no bigger than a match and the other devils would easily blow them out. When he tried to spin a hurricane, it would be but a small breeze they barely noticed; when he called forth a flood, it was barely a trickle.

Even when he was fully grown, his two horns just barely stuck out of his forehead. When he graduated from the University of the Devils, he was determined to do worse than all his classmates, but he soon discovered that many people would not give him a chance. Employers wanted big devils capable of producing major storms, of blowing the tops off volcanoes and shaking the earth. They wanted devils who could make the stock market crash and spread plagues and create great droughts.

Finally the littlest devil found a kindly old devil in the Office of Regional Wars willing to give him a chance to run one region on earth that nobody cared about at all. When wars started there, nobody tried to stop them. Often, nobody even knew that they had started. The pay wasn't good, but for the littlest devil this was the chance he had been waiting for to prove his ability to do really bad things.

He did just as he'd been taught in school: he gave food and shelter to one side and starved the other, he gave guns to the starving side but not to the other side—and then he created a confrontation. And waited.

The result was terrible. The two sides negotiated a peace treaty in which they shared the food and the guns! The littlest devil was fired in shame. People laughed at him and right in front of him said he couldn't even start an argument between a Jew and an Arab.

The littlest devil tried everything he could to make people hate him, but he just couldn't do it. Even the few freelance jobs he got didn't work out well. Once he was hired to create a small tidal wave—and ended up providing the perfect conditions for a surfing competition. Another time he was hired just to make it rain enough to wash out a big golf tournament; but he got his dates mixed up and it rained just in time to make the entire course lush and green when the tournament began.

The littlest devil was so unhappy. He had no fire in his eyes. Maybe he just wasn't cut out to be a devil, he thought, maybe he should go into another profession, maybe he should be a lawyer. But one day, as he was sitting all alone, an old devil saw him there and asked, "What's the problem, young devil?"

"Just everything. Nothing I do turns out bad. Every time I try to create a disaster it turns out to be a disaster. I can't make anybody hate me."

The old devil chuckled. "You know, when I was just getting into this business, I had a similar problem. It seemed like no matter what I did, somehow it turned out wrong. One summer I made this wonderful heat wave, it was hotter than here, and then somebody went and invented air-conditioning. And when I started a flu epidemic, somebody else discovered a flu vaccine. For a time there it was very tough."

The littlest devil was intrigued. "Then what did you do?"

The old devil leaned down and said softly, "That's when I realized you didn't need to do really big things. Those people down there are very clever for human beings. If I did something really big, it got their attention and they did something to stop it. So instead, I started doing small things, and I found that small things eventually become big things, but by the time they do it's too late to stop them."

"Like what?"

"Who do you think made it so easy to get a divorce?" The old devil stood up proudly. "That's right, you're looking at him. By the time they figured it out, it was too late. It was more widespread and affected more people than an epidemic."

The littlest devil looked at him with wonder. And then he set out determined to do some good bad things. Think small, he reminded himself, think very small. And he thought and he thought and he thought, and the smallest thing he could think of was—a tiny flea.

A flea? What harm could he possibly cause with a flea? he wondered. And as much as he thought about it, he couldn't come up with that answer. But sometimes, he realized, he just had to have faith in Satan that things would turn out badly. A flea, he decided firmly, that's how he would get started.

It was a hot summer evening on earth. The littlest devil searched until he found a smiling dog. Then, just as he had learned in Freshmen Spells 101, he pressed all the right buttons and created one small flea. It wasn't much of a flea, but it was a flea. And as the dog was walking down the street, the littlest devil made his flea bite that dog as hard as he possibly could.

The dog yelped and ran into the street.

A car driving down the street swerved to avoid the dog and slammed into a parked car.

The parked car went crashing into a light pole and hit it so hard that it made it almost fall down.

The falling light pole stretched the wires until they tore loose. In the power station, bells went off and all the power going through those wires was diverted to another system.

That other system was already operating at full capacity when the additional power began surging through its wires. This overloaded the system and sparks began flying. The engineers had to shut it down.

But when they shut down this generator, other systems in faraway places that were connected to it also became overloaded and had to be shut down. House by house, street by street, neighborhood by neighborhood, town by town, city by city, state by state, the entire country lost all its power. Lights went out and television sets went dark and refrigerators turned off so all the food inside began melting; computers stopped computing, cordless telephones wouldn't work, and traffic lights blinked off and people drove right through them and had accidents.

All the devils watched this happening. This was truly a terrible thing, they thought, with immense delight. And then they wondered, who could have done such a grand thing? When they learned that this had been the work of the littlest devil, at first they couldn't believe it, no one thought he would ever do anything bad. But finally all the big devils apologized to him and told him that while he might be small in size, he was a very big devil!

The littlest devil was never sad again, for he had learned the most important lesson: bad things can also come in small packages.

—*Steve Boynton*

The Ultimate Salesperson

I DIDN'T INTEND TO BUY A NEW FIFTY-INCH HDTV SET WITH picture-in-picture, VCR, TiTV, Internet connection, DVD, surround-sound stereo, and fax machine. I didn't intend to, that is, until I met Marvin, the single finest salesperson I have ever known. The fact is, I didn't trust salespeople. I thought they were simply out to sell me their product, but Marvin made me feel secure. "I don't know, Marvin," I told him in my wavering voice, "it seems like the day after I buy something the new model comes out and mine is obsolete."

"You are so lucky," Marvin told me. "If you had been here yesterday, somebody would be telling you that today. But this is the new model. It's got input capability for every known broadcast system."

That was impressive. "The truth is, Marvin, I'm not really good at mechanical things. I mean, I can't even tape a program. This . . . this is much too complicated for me."

"Boy, do I know what you mean. Believe me, I

couldn't find north if I was standing on a compass. That's why this is so wonderful. It's a dial system." He handed me a round controller with the names of each feature around a circle. "You just turn the pointer to the feature you want and press the one button. It really is that simple."

He satisfied each of my many doubts. He told me how to get it up the stairs and into my one-bedroom apartment, he arranged financing so cleverly that I wouldn't have to begin paying for it until my first child graduated from college—and I wasn't even engaged. So there was only one more thing that bothered me: quality. "We live in a disposable culture," I said. "With just about everything I own, it costs more to fix it than replace it. And quality just isn't as good as it once was. I'm just afraid I'm going to get it home and within a few years it'll break."

Marvin was shaking his head and smiling. "Can't happen. This is the best-made set in history. This set never breaks. Never. In *Consumer's Digest* tests they ran it the equivalent of thirty-five years and didn't have a single problem. Every part is selected from the finest suppliers in the world. It just doesn't break. Ever. There has never been anything like it."

"I've heard that before," I challenged him. "So what if it does break?"

He smiled proudly. "It comes with a twenty-year guarantee for all parts and labor."

I couldn't believe it. "Every part is guaranteed?"

"Every one. And if you ever have to replace or repair anything, the manufacturer pays for it."

"Every single part? Even the little doohickeys?"

He nodded firmly. "Every single part."

"You mean to tell me that if eight years from now I have a problem with this . . . system, someone'll come to my house and fix it? For free?"

"Even ten years from now. Or twelve years. For the next twenty years this is completely guaranteed. One hundred percent. Every single piece. The big pieces and the small pieces. There is nothing that can go wrong with this set that we won't fix for free. Nada. Zip. You buy it; if it breaks, we repair it."

"Okay, you've sold me. I'll take it!"

This was the moment that I finally appreciated Marvin's greatness as a salesman. "That's terrific, just wonderful. You won't regret it." He paused. "Now, I assume you'll be wanting to purchase the extended warranty?"

—Andrew Fox

Tears of Happiness

No one has to be taught to cry. That's what most people believe. Crying is a natural expression of emotion. Even the smallest baby cries.

But I couldn't. I have no idea what happened to me when I was very young that caused me to repress my feelings, but as I was growing up, I never cried. Never. That made me unhappy. All the other kids seemed to be crying all the time. Eventually my mom became concerned about it. "If you can't cry," she said, "then you can't feel real joy either."

I knew how much my mother loved me when she promised lovingly, "Don't worry, sweetheart, I'll give you something to cry about!"

Her efforts started the very next day. When I came home from school, I found my favorite Barbie doll ripped into pieces. Her arms were on the floor, her legs were on the bed, her head was sitting on my pillow. "Boy, Barbie," I said, "you look pretty silly without your body."

I loved that Barbie, and Mom thought surely this would make me cry. "If you know what's good for you," she warned, "you'll start crying."

I wanted to cry so badly. But every time I could feel myself getting ready to cry, I got so happy that I was finally going to cry that I couldn't.

Mom tried everything she could think of. At dinner she would warn me, "Don't you dare finish everything on your plate." Sometimes we would go to the big shopping mall and she would leave me all alone, knowing that I would be frightened and hoping that might make me cry. One day she got real mad at me for not crying and marched me into the bathroom and flushed my pet goldfish, Heckle and Jeckle, right down the toilet. "There," she said, smiling, "how do you like that!"

As I watched them swirl away, I realized I wouldn't have to remember to feed them every single day and clean the tank. "Bye-bye," I said, waving to the fish.

That only served as a challenge to my mother. And the things she would do to try to make me cry only proved how much she loved me. I'll never forget our little cocker spaniel, Troubles. Troubles was always getting into trouble. He barked all day and all night, he made a mess in the house for Mom to clean up, but I still loved him. Troubles was always there to greet me when I came home from school, his tail waving excitedly knowing we would be going out to play in the yard. We'd play for hours. I would throw the ball and he would fetch it and bring it back to me. But one day when I came home from school, little Troubles wasn't there to greet me. When I asked Mom where he was, she said, "Oh, I hung him in the closet."

Sure enough, there was Troubles, hanging in my closet. That made me angry. "Now I'm gonna have to go fetch the ball myself," I thought.

But I still didn't cry. Sometimes my mom got so frustrated she would yell at me and smack my bottom. "I'll give you something to not cry about!" But that didn't help at all.

My little brother cried a lot. And honestly, I couldn't understand why his crying bothered my mom even more than my not crying, but it really did. And when Mom told me that my little brother had gone away forever, that time I really almost cried. But just as I felt the tears in my eyes, I remembered that I wouldn't have to share my toys anymore. So I still didn't cry.

Finally one day the people in white coats came to take my mom to the hospital. They put her in this funny little jacket and then made her get into the back of the van. As I watched that big van driving away, I felt a single tear running down my face. Now there would be no one there to try to make me cry, and that made me so sad I started to cry. I knew Mom would be so proud of me, and in only ten or fifteen years I would be able to show her.

—*Elaine Johns*

The Last Word

ON THE HILLY PLAINS ABOVE THE HUDSON, ALEXANDER Hamilton stood approximately twelve feet away from rival Aaron Burr. Both men held pistols in their hands, aimed at their opponent, ready to settle their dispute. As the referee dropped his hand to begin the duel, Hamilton pronounced for all the world to hear, "I have not yet begun to fi—"

Thus Hamilton's last words were preserved for posterity. We chronicle the last words of people to learn about them, their courage, and their emotions, as they faced that final encounter. For it is through the choice of these final words that we also learn something about ourselves as a civilization. Cataloging these last recorded words has been a hobby of Caroline Brown's for several years, and her collection currently numbers more than twenty-two thousand. Several of her favorites, chosen for their expression of courage, are included here.

Famed animal trainer Zane Bresloff as he stepped without a gun or a whip into a cage containing nine lions: "Lions are essentially cowards. All you have to do is show them you're not afraid, they'll back down every time. Here, watch this."

Mark Mullis, a lawyer, while driving home from work on the Long Island Expressway: "Of course I can talk on my cell phone while driving this car. Are you kidding me? I can do that with my eyes closed—"

Legendary daredevil Jerry Simon, about to begin the first mountain-climbing expedition of his career: "Mt. Everest, Mt. Schmeverest, they're all the same to me. Just mounds of dirt and rock with snow on the . . . the whatchamacallit, the top thing."

Mike "Just One More" Peterson, after another night on the town: "Trust me, if Superman can do it, I can do itttttttttttttttttttttt . . ."

Philanthropist John J. Sterling III: "Trust me, darling. You don't think I'd make my new, beautiful twenty-four-year-old wife the beneficiary of everything I've worked the last seventy-one years for and then hand her a gun that's loaded."

Carl "Smooth" Jackson: "I'll bet you the five thousand dollars you need to save your house that I can stand directly in front of your car and you don't have the guts to do anything about it."

Sea captain James "Sailor" O'Brian: "Ah, there's nothing I like better than a brisk breeze in the morning."

Pro wrestling fan Herbert Williams, speaking to famed wrestler "The Mad Maniac": "Hey, you fat load. That's right, you. You think you're so tough? You're a fatter phony than the rest of these frauds!"

Stockbroker Ronald G. Harrison speaking to a client: "You're right, it really is too bad that all your Microsoft crashed like that. But, hey, that's the way it goes sometimes. Boy, I'm sure glad I sold all my Microsoft yesterday."

Mrs. Martha Trimble to her husband, Leonard, while camping in Yellowstone Forest: "How many times have I told you not to mumble, Leonard? Ten thousand? A million? Now speak clearly. Did you say there was a steak behind me? Or a snake?"

Richard Baldwin: "So, mister, tie one leg to one car bumper and tie the other leg to another car bumper and drive them in different directions. You really think you scare me?"

Note to Reader

Into each life some poop must fall. If you have had a fitting experience you'd like to share with readers, please e-mail us at *http://www.ChickenPoopfortheSoul.com*. Please include your name and a way to contact you, although we definitely will keep all names confidential.